During the past five years the Society of Publication Designers has enjoyed a tremendous growth, in both membership and prestige. This growth has enabled us to publish this, our first permanent bound annual.

In undertaking this task, we felt that the book should be more than a record of the best in publication design, 1976. Therefore, we have included a comprehensive listing (when available) of contributory credits, allowing the annual to be used as an industry-wide source of information.

Although the material shown is of a higher quality than most past SPD shows, it left me with a strong sense of **déjà vu**. The lack of truly innovative material (for too many years) surprises me on two counts. First, because there are more creative and talented art directors, designers, illustrators and photographers working at the same time than ever before, and, second, because their market is such a huge one. (At last count there were more than 35,000 U.S. publications in existence.)

Whether art or editorial people (or both) can be faulted for this, I cannot say. Perhaps, as in other fields, new breakthroughs out of old patterns are few and far between. Hopefully, in the very near future, a publication (new or old) will come along and knock us over with a completely different and glorious approach.

Until then, don't be put off; the work in this annual is a quite marvelous sampling of the most creative work being done in publications today. So scan it . . . study it . . . enjoy it!

Ira Silberlicht
President 1976-1977

Publication Design 12

The Society of Publication Designers
3 West 51st Street, New York, New York 10019

OFFICERS 1977-1978

John Barban, *President,* Science Digest
Elizabeth-Anne Wilbur, *Vice-President,* American Heritage
Noel Werritt, *Vice President,* Quest '77
Jack Golden, *Treasurer,* Designers 3
Ezra Shapiro, *Secretary,* Free Enterprise

BOARD OF DIRECTORS 1977-1978

Murray Belsky, American Heritage Publishing
Victor Closi, Field & Stream
John Conley, The Lamp (Exxon)
Robert Essman, People
Robert Herald, Hospital Practice
Philip Ritzenberg, New York News
Ira Silberlicht, Consulting Art Director/Designer
Louis Silverstein, New York Times

The Society of Publication Designers wishes
to thank the following individuals
for their assistance in preparing this book:

Design — Elizabeth-Anne Wilbur
General Assistance — Nancy Cutler
Cover Illustration — Bill Nelson
Award Photographs — Tom Yahashi
Index — Mary Tomaselli

CONTENTS

JUDGES

Donald A. Adamec, Ladies Home Journal
Tom Bodkin, C.B.S., Inc.
Joe Brooks, Penthouse Magazine
Aaron Burns, International Typeface Corporation
JoAnne Cassella, Medical Economics
Vincent Ceci, MacMillan Professional Magazines
Ivan Chermayeff, Chermayeff & Geismar Associates
Robert Clive, New York News Magazine
George Coderre, Reinhold Publishing Co.
Bob Crozier, Bob Crozier Enterprises
Ken Cunningham, Weight Watchers Magazine
Herb Cytryn, McGraw-Hill, Inc.
John DeCesare, Ciba-Geigy Pharmaceuticals
Barbara Devine, Today's Secretary
Madlyn W. Dickens, MacMillan Book Clubs
Henry Epstein, American Broadcasting Co.
A. Bryan Fisher, Communication Magazine
Alberto P. Gavasci, Interior Design Publications
Campbell Geeslin, People Magazine
Irwin Glusker, Irwin Glusker Studio
Mike Gross, Mobil Corporation
Emma Landau, American Heritage
Jonathan Larsen, New Times Magazine
David C. Levy, Parsons School of Design
Bob Melson, The New York Times
James O'Bryan, National Review
Steve Phillips, New Times Magazine
Howard Ravis, Folio
Joe Sapinsky, Woman's Day Magazine
Tamara Schneider, Seventeen Magazine
Neil Shakery, Psychology Today
David Starwood, Arthur Young Journal
Herbert Taylor, Spectrum
Shirley Tomkievicz
John R. Vogler, Business Week
Jack Wolff, Adjunct Ltd.
Carmile Zaino, American Heritage Publishing Co.
Ron Zisman, Backpacker Magazine

**A. Bryan Fisher
Art Director,
Communication Magazine
New Jersey Bell**

The opportunity to create good design is a heady experience, rarely afforded to those who must work for a living.

Yet those of us who design publications on a regular basis seldom take the time to step back from our work, look around and acknowledge this unusual good fortune.

Perhaps the reason for this crass oversight is the inevitable sense of guilt which descends on one who realizes he is being paid to do something for which, under different circumstances, he might be willing to forfeit some money to enjoy the experience.

Guilt may not be the correct word for the feeling. It's more akin to the exhilaration of the successful party crasher or that combination of fright and delight a kid gets when he sneaks into the movies.

The party we are crashing or the movie we are sneaking into is an awesome spectacle, indeed. The designer's art is a fearsome apparition consuming the best ideas of those who tackle it at an appalling rate. And the ability of the gifted to satisfy this voracious appetite is perhaps the most impressive thing one can cite when commenting on the state of publication design today.

Moreover, it's pleasing to note that tidbits from the semi-gifted are devoured with equal relish so long as they are salted with honest effort and coated with a little sauce.

The demand for quality work has never been higher and the resultant opportunities have never been greater.

Designing a publication is a bold act of ego. In addition to creating and offering tidbits, designers must constantly avoid being crushed by falling deadlines and are often required to hurtle the chasm created by an open page in the book. Still, egotistical as we are, there are few of us who don't savor the challenge and welcome the privilege.

And now, if you'll excuse me, I have to go feed the monster.

Neil Shakery was art director of Psychology Today Magazine. He is now a partner in the design firm of Jonson, Pedersen and Hinrichs.

By now I'm sure we all share the feeling that the seventies has been a period when our collective creative juices have been at a low ebb. Look at music, fine art, movies. Pick your own favorite area of concern and the feeling is there, unmistakably. That publication design is no exception was forcefully brought to mind in judging this Society of Publication Designers show.

Going through piles of entries was a frustrating process. I saw a lot of retrenching, tired variations on already overused ideas, copies of copies of copies. What I didn't see was much that was fresh or daring or perhaps even downright terrible. What I saw was a dreadful sameness. Sameness not only of design but of illustration, of photography and of concept. It was almost as though all of these publications had been shaken out of some huge grab bag of material and none emerged with much personality. Even new magazines with a chance to start afresh often reneged and latched onto a format that somebody else had used before successfully.

The fact that all magazines are now the same size and shape and are printed on the same crappy paper of course is a contributing factor, but I think there is much more to it than that. Some magazines that emerged fresh and vital a few years ago now seem content to do poorly what they once did with style and purpose. The underground press, being no longer underground, has run itself into a dead end which no longer holds much interest. Many consumer magazines that adopted trash design inspired by the ingenuousness of the underground press didn't have the wit to know when to let go. They have institutionalized what was once a valid reaction to the mainstream and turned it into something tedious and long past its usefulness.

What I feel we need desperately is a point of inspiration, a touchstone to hold our work up to on a day to day basis. Since there is no publication that seems to be fulfilling that role at present, I wish the Society of Publication Designers exhibition and annual could do so, but I am afraid it will fall very far short.

What I regret about judging this show is that so much really mediocre work will be included merely to meet the reality of filling the walls of the gallery and pages of the annual. I think we should go beyond merely recording who did what when and try to set some standards to live by as designers.

There is not much inspiration for the designers of next year to be found in the work of last year in the current Society of Publication Designers show. This was not a vintage year for publication design.

Campbell Geeslin
Senior Editor
People Magazine

For many decades the look of a newspaper was determined by the machinery. Hot type was set in columns. Design was dictated pretty much by technology. We came to expect newspapers to have a certain appearance. When offset printing and computer-set photo composition took over, its developers assumed that everyone wanted the new to imitate the old. Caxton set his type ragged on the right, too.

Isn't it time for designers who understand the new technology to step in, examine the possibilities, and see if it is necessary for us to continue obsolete hot type restrictions in the production of publications?

Catalogs may be the best art directed publications around because a reader looks at them completely unaware that the business of art direction has taken place. The art isn't just decorative. It shows, in as detailed a manner as possible, a product that is being offered for sale. It must look attractive, or no one will want to buy it, and yet it mustn't be so far from the truth that a buyer will feel deceived when the merchandise arrives.

The copy is always to the point, too —information with a minimum of fuss. It too is prepared with one thing in mind: to give a reader the information he needs to buy the product so clearly, accurately and alluringly presented in artwork or photograph.

The complex relationship between television and publishing is fun to watch. Television has not, as once was feared, killed off newspapers, magazines and books. Mini-series from books proliferate on TV, and then viewers go out and buy the books on which they are based.

Television producers keep trying to put together shows they call a "magazine" with "feature articles" about people or events that are neither news documentaries nor fictional dramas. How much has quick-image television with its clever, information-packed commercials inspired magazines to change? That is, give readers lots of photographs with small amounts of text? Is there such a thing as a magazine for people who prefer to watch television?

Stop off in front of a big newsstand in one of the uptown buildings and try to absorb the extraordinary chaos. Try to make sense of the assault on the eye's retina.

There is a staggering proliferation of beautiful color, especially reds and yellows. (Do they indeed grab the attention first?) There are splendid photographs, flashes of flesh, skillful art, familiar famous faces and attention-grabbing words: LOVE, SEX, MONEY, BIG, BOLD . . . The whole mass of covers adds up to an incredibly inventive depiction of what we are today.

These displays change slightly from week to week and, once each month, a larger shift takes place. In the spring the colors are greens and pinks. With the approach of summer the shades will become sunny yellows and oranges. And in the fall, just like leaves in the woods, the whole newsstand will turn to browns and golden shades.

Magazine covers are not created by attic-starving recluses. They are produced by art directors and artists whose very livelihood depends on how successfully they can catch the fancy of the passerby. Every cover is out there to attract, to please as many viewers as it possibly can.

And so we are today revealed. Our ideal beautiful woman is no longer a Botticelli angel. It's Farrah Fawcett-Majors, a television angel. The insides of our homes are filled with flower-printed furnishings. We are enamored of money deals and quantities of skin. We love shiny, expensive cars and gadgets.

What do our art museums say? The Metropolitan offers ancient history. The Museum of Modern Art is decades behind what's happening today.

The real museums of contemporary life and art are newsstands. Magazines, in racks from floor to ceiling, in stacks, displayed and begging for our approval are the only accurate depiction of our immediate concerns. It's absorbing and totally relevant. Stop off at your neighborhood newsstand and take a good look at yourself.

James W. O'Bryan,
Art Director
National Review

Aside from the usual excellence of the entries, I discerned very few pieces I would consider either avant-garde or trend setting. I don't feel this is unusual, however, since too often good design is censored. The illustrations, although mostly top-notch, seemed to fall well within the current norms of acceptability.

Predictably, newspapers covered the Bi-Centennial in many of their entries. Although this particular medium imposes design limitations that can be difficult to deal with, I was pleasantly surprised to see a greater emphasis on type and photo design as well as some interesting picture cropping. I consider this to be a refreshing trend for designers and/or art directors who may finally be exercising a stronger voice in what newspaper should or could look like.

I discerned no trends at all in the entries that featured photography. In retrospect, perhaps photography was more strongly represented than illustration, but my feeling is that these entries lacked the artistry that is possible in photography. Some of the best photography I recall viewing appeared in a few of the corporate annual reports. The photographing of concepts was excellent, but I attribute this more to the skill of the designers' concepts than to that of the photographers.

The technical publications were all neatly designed typographically . . . clean, good taste, judicious use of white space, not gaudy. But where they need an "operation boot strap" is in their charts, graphs and technical illustrations. For the most part, these were done in the most primitive way, but in four colors. A greater effort in this area would vastly improve the appearance of their publications.

When I look around, I see so many poorly designed products —ads, buildings, automobiles, etc. —yet, I know our professionals are not lacking in talent. It therefore has to be said that someone *else* is the arbiter of taste. When we begin to take advantage of all the new technology available to designers (i.e. photo machines, typositors, film techniques, computers, etc.), I predict we will then be making that quantum leap into the new age of design.

John deCesare
Executive Art Director
Geigy-Pharmaceuticals

Always, the winner, the innovative, the beautiful, the concerned, the new, the provocative presented themselves without destroying the orchestration of the whole— the magazine, the newspaper of America today.

As it always will be, I suppose, the old (illustration techniques in this case) attempt to wipe off the dust and cobwebs to take position on shaky legs alongside the exciting three-dimensional plastic creations of the graphic entertainers of today.

It seems to me the specialty magazine has forced the essential cooperation between editor and art director/designer to the satisfaction of the reader and assured media for the advertiser.

The lack of dynamic interest in the newspaper area is disturbing. People love newspapers—each day they offer opportunities not available to magazines.

George W. Coderre
Art Director
Reinhold Publishing Company

In judging this year's Society of Publication Designers' Show, I could not help but sense a tremendous range of graphic effort. Some excellent, some almost totally insensitive. This range seemed to occur in all areas, including typography, photography and illustration. However, those publications that are well done—are well done issue after issue. Seldom does the level fall. Similarly, those that are poorly done are poorly done time after time.

Those publications that are done well are done so regardless of size, color limitations, etc. A well done B/W publication is still, and always will be, attractive. Example—The New York Times. Realizing their limitations, they are certainly pioneers in the handling of B/W. A sensitive choice of art, combined with editorial yields a superb effort.

Others try to fool us, using a second color arbitrarily or 4-color badly. Color is not in itself exciting; rather, it is how it is used. The same holds true for photography and art. And it takes no more effort to put type together intelligently than badly.

Attractive, inviting, challenging publication design is certainly being done. Not enough of it, though, for it seems clear that "All publications are not created equal."

JEROME SNYDER AWARD

This special "Best-of-Show" award is to honor the memory of Jerome Snyder, whose talent, wit and energy have inspired so many art directors and designers through the years.

The award recognizes exceptional art direction in overall design of a publication, *the ultimate achievement,* and is awarded each year that the judges believe an entry merits it. It is the highest honor the Society can confer upon an art director, and is intended to inspire the members of our profession to greater heights of excellence.

The award for 1976, presented to the art director/designer team Stuart Silver and Alvin Grossman, was for **American Ephemera,** the publication of the Metropolitan Museum of Art in New York City.

The Master Eagle Gallery
40 West 25th Street, New York, NY 10010 · 6th Floor

AWARDS OF EXCELLENCE

Title: American Ephemera
Art Director: Stuart Silver
Designer: Al Grossman
Illustrator: Museum Collections
Photographer: Museum Studios

Typesetter: York Typographers
Color Separator: Sanders Printing
Printer: Sanders Printing
Paper Manufacturer: Warren Paper Co.

Title: Emergency Medicine
Art Directors: Ira Silberlicht, Tom Lennon
Designers: Tom Lennon, Irving J. Cohen
Photographer: Shig Ikeda

Typesetter: Allied Typographers. Inc.
Color Separator: Electronic Step and Repeat
Printer: Lincoln Graphic Arts, Inc.
Paper Manufacturer: Crown Zellerbach Corp.

Title: Hoof Beats
Art Director: Jan V. White
Designer: Jan V. White
Photographer: George Smallsreed

Typesetter: Watkins Printing Company
Color Separator: Stevenson Photocolor Co.
Printer: Watkins Printing Company
Paper Manufacturer: Mead Papers

Title: Kodak International Photography
Art Directors: Kenn Jacobs and Erwin Ritenis
Designer: Erwin Ritenis
Photographer: Various

Typesetter: Rochester Monotype Inc.
Color Separator: Rochester Polychrome Press. Great Lakes Press
Printer: Rochester Polychrome Press. Great Lakes Press
Paper Manufacturer: Northwest Paper Company

Title: Playboy
Art Director: Arthur Paul
Designer: Len Willis
Illustrator: Kunio Hagio
Printer: W. E. Hall

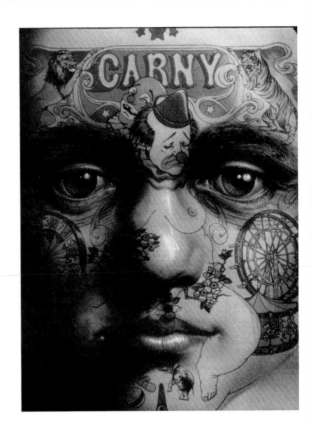

Title: Quest 77   **Color Separator:** R. R. Donnelley
Art Director: Noel Werrett   **Printer:** R. R. Donnelley
Designer: Noel Werrett   **Paper Manufacturer:** Westvaco
Typesetter: Cardinal Type

Title: The Arthur Young Journal
Art Director: David Starwood
Designer: Will Martin
Photographers: Don Jim, Lee Boltin, Beverly Peterson
Typesetter: Boro
Printer: S. D. Scott

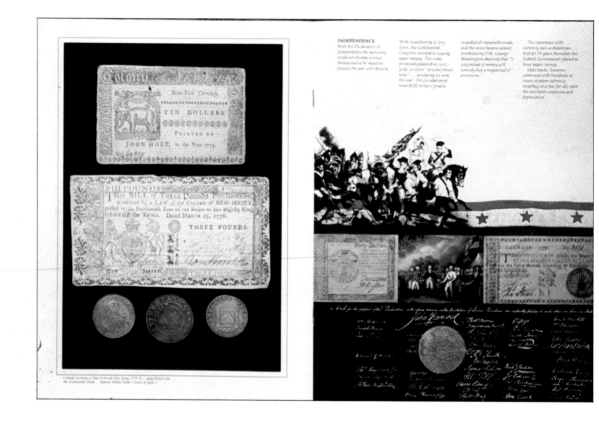

Title: California Business
Art Director: Bob Kinkead
Designer: Bob Kinkead

Title: U & lc
Art Director: Herb Lubalin
Designer: Herb Lubalin
Illustrator: Jerome Snyder

Typesetter: Photo Lettering, Inc.
Printer: Lincoln Graphic Arts, Inc.
Paper Manufacturer: Great Northern

AWARDS OF DISTINCTIVE MERIT

Title: AIA Journal
Art Director: Suzy Thomas
Designer: Suzy Thomas
Photographer: Patricia Duncan
Typesetter: Hodges
Color Separator: Falcon
Printer: Judd & Detweiler
Paper Manufacturer: Westvaco

Title: American Ephemera
Art Director: Stuart Silver
Designer: Al Grossman
Illustrator: Museum Collections
Photographer: Museum Studios
Typesetter: York Typographers
Color Separator: Sanders Printing
Printer: Sanders Printing
Paper Manufacturer: Warren Paper Co.

Title: Emergency Medicine
Art Directors: Ira Silberlicht, Tom Lennon
Designer: Tom Lennon
Illustrator: Judith Jampel
Photographer: Eugenia Louis
Typesetter: Allied Typographers, Inc.
Color Separator: Electronic Step and Repeat
Printer: Perry Printing Corp.
Paper Manufacturer: Crown Zellerbach Corp.

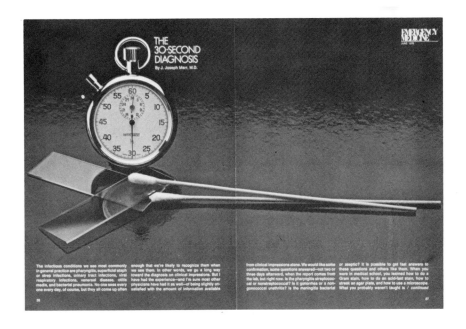

Title: Emergency Medicine
Art Director: Ira Silberlicht, Tom Lennon
Designer: Tom Lennon
Photographer: Shig Ikeda
Typesetter: Allied Typographers, Inc.
Color Separator: Electronic Step and Repeat
Printer: Perry Printing Corp.
Paper Manufacturer: Crown Zellerbach Corp.

Title: Sunday Plain Dealer Magazine
Art Director: Edward Freska
Designer: Nick Dankovich

Title: Family Circle
Art Director: John Bradford
Designer: John Bradford
Illustrator: Paul Sawyer

Photographer: Lynn St. John
Typesetter: Haber Typographers, Inc.
Color Separator: R. R. Donnelley
Printer: R. R. Donnelley

Title: Horizon
Art Director: Ken Munowitz
Designer: Ken Munowitz
Typesetter: The Composing Room
Color Separator: Chanticleer Press
Printer: W. A. Krueger Co
Paper Manufacturer: Mead Papers

Title: Horizon
Art Director: Ken Munowitz
Designer: Ken Munowitz
Typesetter: The Composing Room of New England
Color Separator: Chanticleer Press
Printer: W. A. Krueger
Paper Manufacturer: Mead Papers & Allied Paper Co.

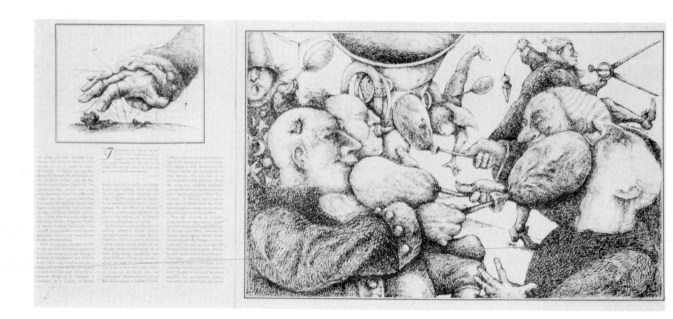

Title: Kodak International Photography
Art Directors: Kenn Jacobs, Erwin Ritenis
Designer: Erwin Ritenis
Photographer: Various
Typesetter: Rochester Monotype Inc.
Color Separator: Rochester Polychrome Press
Printer: Rochester Polychrome Press Inc.
Paper Manufacturer: Northwest Paper Co.

The painted ladies of Serge Lutens

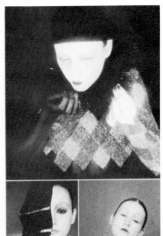

LET THE BUYER BEHOLD!

Title: The Lamp
Art Director: Harry O. Diamond
Designer: Harry O. Diamond
Photographer: Co Rentmeester
Typesetter: Tri-Arts Press, Inc.
Color Separator: The Case-Hoyt Corp
Printer: The Case-Hoyt Corp
Paper Manufacturer: Warren Paper

Title: The Lamp
Art Director: Harry O. Diamond
Designer: Harry O. Diamond
Photographer: David Moore
Typesetter: Tri-Arts Press, Inc.
Color Separator: The Case-Hoyt Corp
Printer: The Case-Hoyt Corp
Paper Manufacturer: Warren Paper

Title: McCall's
Art Director: Alvin Grossman
Designer: Alvin Grossman
Photographer: Bill Binzen

Title: McCalls
Art Director: Alvin Grossman
Designer: Alvin Grossman
Photographer: Otto Storch

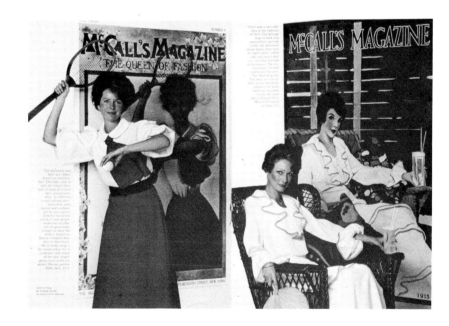

Title: LI (Newsday)
Art Director: Clifford Gardiner
Illustrator: Gary Viskuipic
Printer: Providence Gravure

Title: Living
Art Directors: George Cowan, Bob Ciano &
Louis Silverstein
Designer: Various
Illustrator: Various

Photographer: The New York Times
Typesetter: The New York Times
Printer: The New York Times

Title: New York News Magazine
Art Director: Robert Clive
Designer: Robert Clive
Illustrator: Bruce Stark
Typesetter: New York News
Color Separator: New York News
Printer: New York News

Title: New York News Magazine
Art Director: Robert Clive
Designer: Thomas P. Ruis
Photographer: Tom Arma
Typesetter: New York News
Color Separator: New York News
Printer: New York News

Title: Oui
Art Director: Don Menell
Designer: Jean-Pierre Holley
Illustrator: Guy Fery
Printer: World Color Press

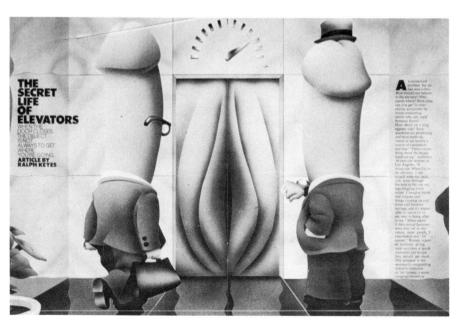

Title: Oui
Art Director: Don Menell
Designer: Don Menell
Illustrator: Robert Grossman
Printer: World Color Press

Title: Popular Photography
Art Director: Shinichiro Tora
Designer: Shinichiro Tora
Photographer: Ralph Gibson

Title: Surgical Techniques Illustrated
Art Director: Clif Gaskill
Designer: Clif Gaskill

Illustrators: Frank Robinson, Carol Donner, Vittorio Fornasari, Albert Teoli, Robert H. Albertin, Paul Singh-Roy, Charles D. Wood, Douglas Cramer, Robert Mohr, Robert Bickford

Typesetter: Monotype Composition
Printer: Halliday Lithograph
Paper Manufacturer: S. D. Warren

Title: Horticulture
Art Director: Bruce McIntosh
Designer: Bruce McIntosh
Illustrators: MHS Library, Mary Purcell
Typesetter: Composing Room
Printer: R. R. Donnelley
Paper Manufacturer: Blandin

Title: Rolling Stone
Art Director: Roger Black
Designers: Richard Avedon, Elizabeth Paul, Roger Black
Photographer: Richard Avedon
Typesetter: MacKenzie & Harris
Printer: Mid-America Printing

Title: Town & Country
Art Director: Linda Stillman
Designer: Brad Pallas
Photographer: Silano
Printer: Meredith Printing Corp.

BY DON VORDERMAN · PHOTOGRAPHS BY SILANO

THE NEW
CARS

Title: U & lc
Art Director: Herb Lubalin
Designer: Herb Lubalin
Illustrators: Geoffrey Moss. Sam Fink. Erte, Jerome Snyder.
 Marie Michal, Alexa Grace, Joseph Pomerance.
 Seymour Chwast, Lou Myers, John Alcorn,
 Marguerita Bornstein, Ann Raymo
Photographers: Simon Cherpital Alfred Gescheidt
Typesetter: LSC&P Design Group, Inc., M. J. Baumwell,
 Photo Lettering, Inc.
Color Separator: Pioneer Moss Reproductions
Printer: Lincoln Graphic Arts, Inc.
Paper Manufacturer: Great Northern Manufacturing Co.

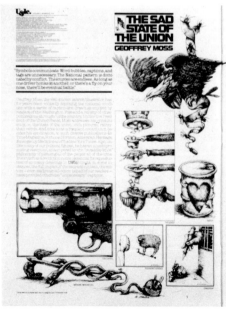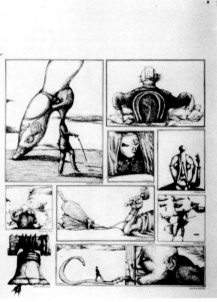

Title: U & lc
Art Director: Herb Lubalin
Designer: Herb Lubalin
Illustrator: Jerome Snyder
Typesetter: Photo Lettering, Inc.
Printer: Lincoln Graphic Arts, Inc.
Paper Manufacturer: Great Northern

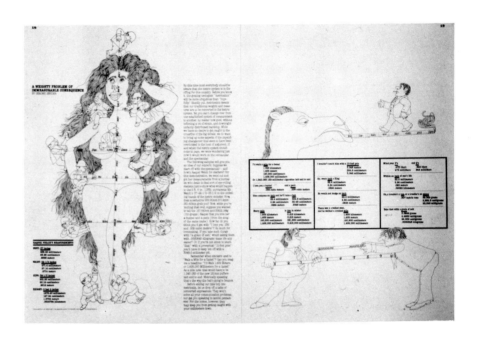

Title: U & lc
Art Director: Herb Lubalin
Designer: Herb Lubalin
Photographer: Alfred Gescheidt
Typesetter: M. J. Baumwell
Printer: Lincoln Graphic Arts, Inc.
Paper Manufacturer: Great Northern

AWARDS OF MERIT

Total Unit Design — Overall

Title: Southwestern Art
Art Director: Larry Smitherman
Designer: Larry Smitherman
Typesetter: Pond Typesetting
Color Separator: Wallace Engraving Company
Publication Printer: The Whitley Company
Paper Manufacturer: Curtis/Weyerhauser/Beckett/
Strathmore/Northwest

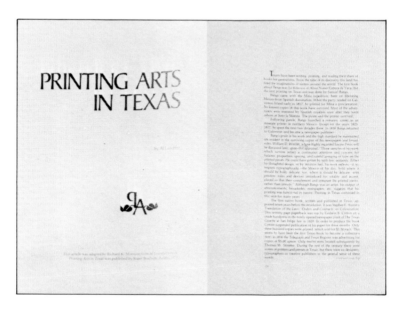

Title: Architectural Digest
Art Director: Philip Kaplan
Designers: Philip Kaplan, Charles Ross
Photographer: Various
Typesetter: Computer Typesetting and Vernon Simpson,
          Los Angeles
Color Separator: J. William Reed Company, Alexandria, Va.
Publication Printer: The Case-Hoyt Corporation
Paper Manufacturer: S. D. Warren

Title: Rolling Stone
Art Director: Roger Black
Designers: Roger Black, Greg Scott
Typesetter: Mackenzie & Harris
Color Separator: Rolling Stone
Publication Printer: Mid-America Printing

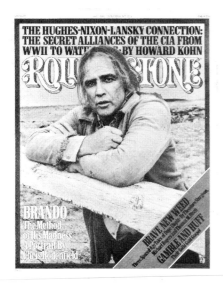

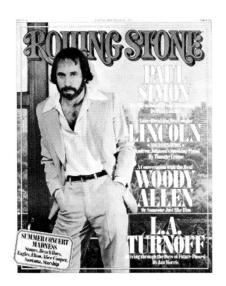

Title: Living
Art Directors: George Cowan, Bob Ciano &
                   Louis Silverstein
Designer: Various
Illustrator: Various
Photographer: The New York Times
Typesetter: The New York Times
Printer: The New York Times

Title: L. I. - Newsday Magazine
Art Director: Clifford Gardiner
Publication Printer: Providence Gravure

The Fulfilling Life For Women at Home

Some women choose to stay home and raise a family instead of going out to get a job. They find there's time to develop personal interests, too.

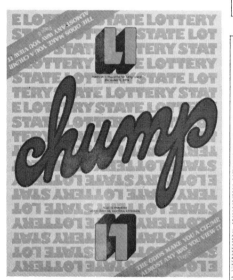

It's a Sucker's Bet, But . . .

The state lottery provides cheap thrills and terrible odds. Yet for this writer, the game is a surefire ticket to good, clean mindless fun.

Title: Sunday News Magazine
Art Director: Robert Clive
Designers: Richard Mozzanica, Thomas P. Ruis
Photographers: Thomas Arma, Ken Korotkin, Roy Morsch
Typesetter: N. Y. News
Color Separator: N. Y. News/Authenticolor
Publication Printer: N. Y. News

Title: Sunday News Magazine
Art Director: Robert Clive
Designers: Richard Mozzanica, Thomas P. Ruis
Photographers: Thomas Arma, Ken Korotkin, Roy Morsch
Typesetter: N. Y. News
Color Separator: N. Y. News/Authenticolor
Publication Printer: N. Y. News

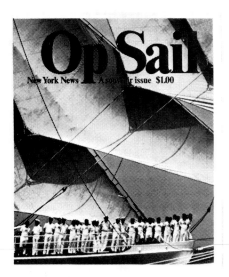

Title: Surgical Techniques Illustrated
Art Director: Clif Gaskill
Designer: Clif Gaskill
Illustrators: Frank Robinson, Carol Donner, Vittorio
    Fornasari, Albert Teoli, Robert H. Albertin,
    Paul Singh-Roy, Charles D. Wood, Douglas Cramer,
    Robert Mohr, Robert Bickford
Typesetter: Monotype Composition Company
Printer: Halliday Lithograph Corporation
Paper Manufacturer: S. D. Warren Company

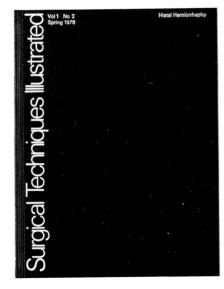

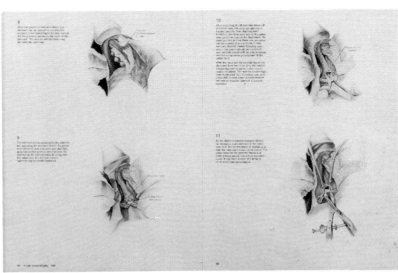

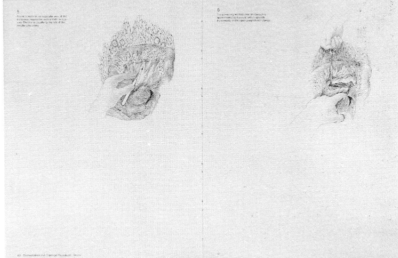

Title: AIA Journal
Art Director: Suzy Thomas
Designer: Suzy Thomas
Typesetter: Hodges
Color Separator: Falcon
Publication Printer: Judd & Detweiler

Title: Medical Student
Art Director: Burton P. Pollack
Designer: Elizabeth R. Cash
Illustrator: Paul J. Singh-Roy
Photographer: Black Star
Typesetter: Robert Guman—"Photographic Productions"
Color Separator: City Printing
Publication Printer: City Printing
Paper Manufacturer: NorthWest

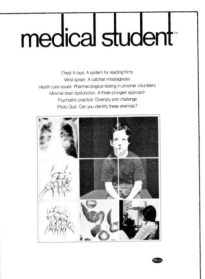

medical student™

Chest X-rays: A system for reading films
Wrist sprain: A catchall misdiagnosis
Health care issues: Pharmacological testing in prisoner volunteers
Minimal brain dysfunction: A three-pronged approach
Psychiatric practice: Diversity and challenge
Photo Quiz: Can you identify these anemias?

Chest X-rays

A system for reading films

By Abner M. Landry, MD

Dr. Landry is clinical assistant professor of radiology, Louisiana State University Medical School, and director of radiology, Mercy Hospital, New Orleans, Louisiana.

The chest X-ray is one of the most important examinations in diagnostic radiology and certainly in lung disease evaluation. However, it is too often taken for granted, both by physicians and patients. In fact, proper study of a chest X-ray is a highly sophisticated and complex task that many radiologists feel should not be undertaken by other physicians unless they seek radiologic consultation.

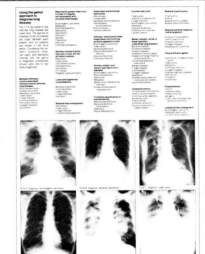

medical student™

Chronic lung disease: Cutting through the complexities
Bone marrow aspiration: One physician's technique
Career planning: Electing a subspecialty
Health care issues: Contemporary drug development
Cardiac dysrhythmias: Five questions point to initial control

Bone marrow aspiration

One physician's technique

By Roland G. Hiss, MD

Dr. Hiss is associate professor of internal medicine and professor of postgraduate medicine at the University of Michigan, Ann Arbor, where he also serves as director of the Office of Educational Resources.

Examination of the bone marrow is an important element in the evaluation process in clinical hematology. When coupled with a critical review of the peripheral blood film, bone marrow examination represents the definitive biopsy for many hematologic diseases and yields accessory useful information for several others.

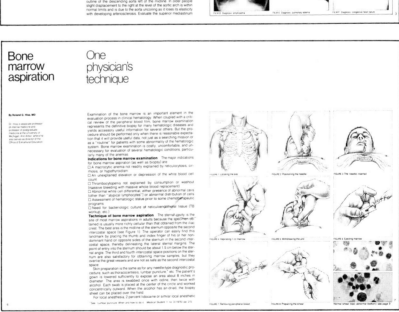

Title: U & lc
Art Director: Herb Lubalin
Designer: Herb Lubalin
Illustrators: Various
Photographers: Various
Typesetter: Photolettering Inc., TGC, M. J. Baumwell LSC&P
                  Design Group Inc.
Color Separator: Pioneer Moss Reproductions
Publication Printer: Lincoln Graphic Arts, Inc.
Paper Manufacturer: Great Northern Manufacturing Co.

Title: Kodak International Photography
Art Directors: Kenn Jacobs, Erwin Ritenis
Designer: Erwin Ritenis
Photographer: Various
Typesetter: Rochester Monotype Inc.
Color Separator: Rochester Polychrome Press Inc.
Publication Printer: Rochester Polychrome Press Inc.
Paper Manufacturer: Northwest Paper Co.

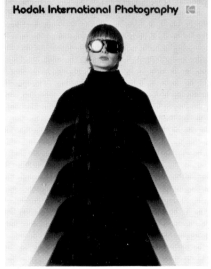

Title: The Lamp
Art Director: Harry O. Diamond
Designer: Harry O. Diamond
Typesetter: Tri-Arts Press, Inc.
Color Separator: The Case-Hoyt Corporation
Publication Printer: The Case-Hoyt Corporation
Paper Manufacturer: S. D. Warren Co.

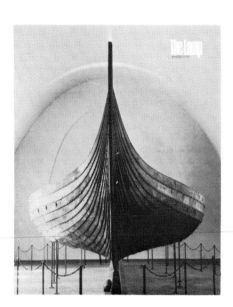

Title: The Arthur Young Journal   **Typesetter:** Johnson/Kenro, Boro
Art Director: David Starwood   **Publication Printer:** S. D. Scott
Designer: David Starwood

Title: Eskalith Newsletter
Art Directors: Alan J. Klawans, Margaret Hawley
Designers: David Stencler, Robin-Hotchkiss, Jack Freas,
Jerome Kaplan, Alan Klawans
Typesetter: W. T. Armstrong
Color Separator: Butler & Ferigno
Publication Printer: Butler & Ferigno
Paper Manufacturer: Weyerhauser

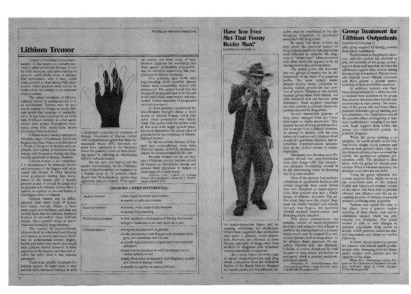

Title: Rolling Stone
Art Director: Roger Black
Designers: Richard Avedon, Elizabeth Paul, Roger Black
Photographer: Richard Avedon
Typesetter: MacKenzie & Harris
Printer: Mid-America Printing

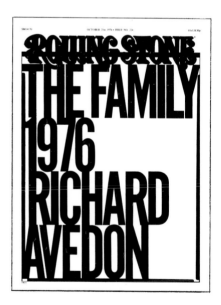

Title: Oui
Art Director: Don Menell
Designer: Don Menell
Publication Printer: World Color Press

Title: Town & Country
Art Director: Linda Stillman
Designers: Linda Stillman, Brad Pallas, Toni Kapcio
Publication Printer: Meredith Printing Corp.

Title: Horizon
Art Director: Ken Munowitz
Designer: Ken Munowitz
Typesetter: The Composing Room of New England

Color Separator: Chanticleer Press
Printer: W. A. Krueger
Paper Manufacturer: Mead Papers & Allied Paper Co.

Title: Orange Express
Art Director: Carl T. Herrman
Designers: Don Trousdell, Vince Maiello
Illustrator: Dagmar Frinta
Typesetter: Cheap Type
Publication Printer: Lakeside Press

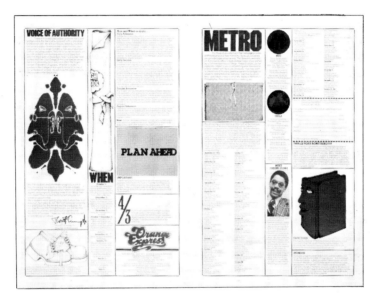

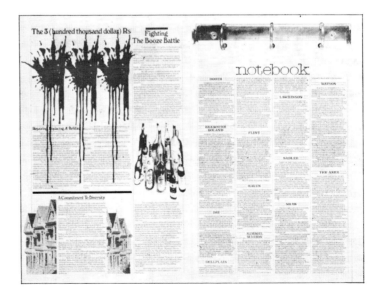

Title: Roomer
Art Director: Artie Lahr
Designer: Artie Lahr
Illustrator: Artie Lahr
Typesetter: Cheap Type
Publication Printer: Lakeside Press

Title: L. I. - Newsday Magazine
Art Director: Clifford Gardiner
Publication Printer: Providence Gravure

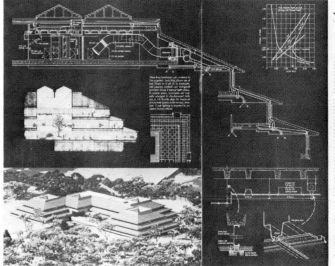

Title: Architectural Record
Art Director: Alex Stillano
Designer: Jan White
Typesetter: Judd & Detweiler
Color Separator: National Colorgraphics
Publication Printer: Judd & Detweiler

Title: Sunday News Magazine
Art Director: Robert Clive
Designer: Richard Mozzanica
Photographers: Roy Morsch, Thomas P. Ruis, Peter Kaplan,
Burt Glinn, Richard Kalvar, A. J. Levin,
Harry Hamburg, Vincent Riehl, Burt Miller,
Mark Godfrey, Fred Conrad

Typesetter: N. Y. News
Color Separator: Authenticolor
Publication Printer: N. Y. News

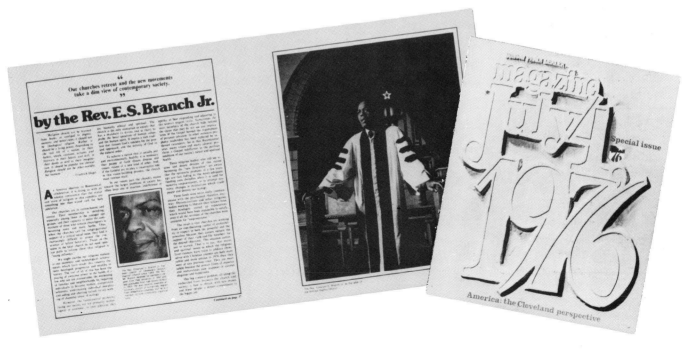

Title: The Plain Dealer Magazine
Art Director: Edward Freska
Designer: Edward Freska
Illustrator: Edward Freska
Photographer: Robert Dorksen
Typesetter: Art Gravure Corp. of Ohio
Color Separator: Art Gravure Corp. of Ohio
Publication Printer: Art Gravure Corp. of Ohio

Title: Regional Design Assembly
Art Director: James E. Johnson
Designer: James E. Johnson
Illustrator: James E. Johnson
Typesetter: Mono-Trade Co.
Publication Printer: Johnson Printing Co.

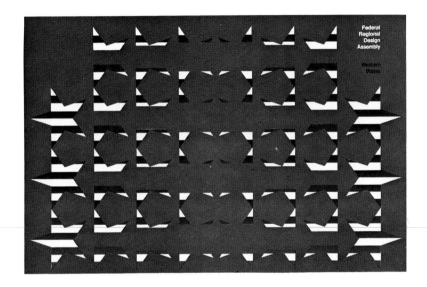

Title: Mainliner
Art Director: Kathy Philpott
Designer: Kathy Philpott
Typesetter: Computer Typesetting Service & RS
                Typographics
Color Separator: Lithatone
Publication Printer: Deseret Press
Paper Manufacturer: Crown Zellerbach

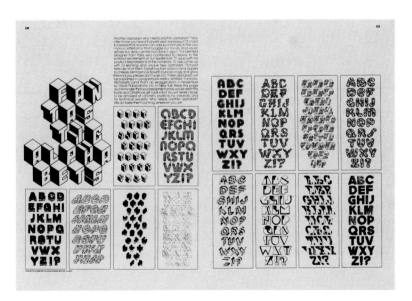

Title: U & lc
Art Director: Herb Lubalin
Designer: Herb Lubalin
Illustrators: Lou Myers, John Alcorn,
  Marguerita Bornstein, Ann Raymo

Photographers: Simon Cherpitel, Alfred Gescheidt
Typesetter: Photo Lettering Inc., TGC, M. J. Baumwell
Publication Printer: Lincoln Graphic Arts, Inc.
Paper Manufacturer: Great Northern Manufacturing Co.

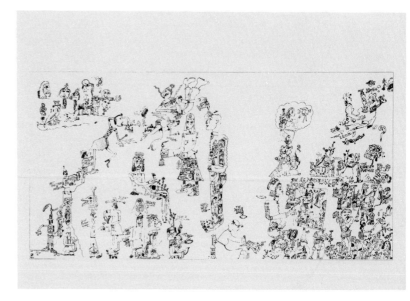

Title: U & lc
Art Director: Herb Lubalin
Designer: Herb Lubalin
Illustrators: Seymour Chwast, Jerome

Snyder, Marie Michal, Alexa Grace, Joseph Pomerance
Typesetter: M. J. Baumwell, Photo Lettering, Inc.
Color Separator: Lincoln Graphic Arts, Inc.
Paper Manufacturer: Great Northern Manufacturing Co.

Title: Design Quarterly '76
Art Director: James E. Johnson
Designer: James E. Johnson
Illustrator: James E. Johnson
Typesetter: Mono-Trade Co. Minneapolis
Color Separator: Color-House Minneapolis
Publication Printer: Kolor Press Minneapolis

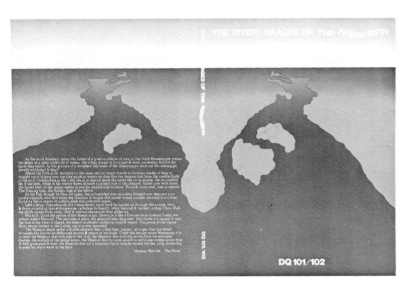

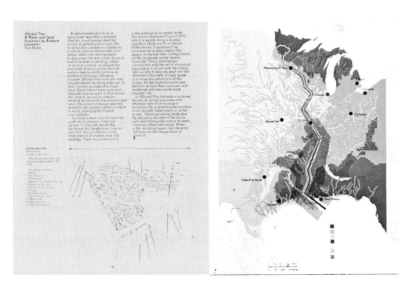

Title: The Men & Machines That Made America
Art Director: Jim Naughton
Designers: Ed Dahl, Trez Cattie
Illustrator: Assorted Historical Paintings & Wood cuts
Typesetter: Chilton
Color Separator: Gilbert Color
Publication Printer: Chilton Printing
Paper Manufacturer: Champion

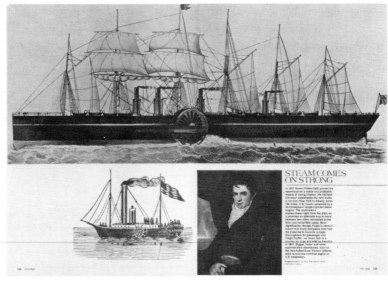

Title: The Summer Times
Art Director: Carl T. Herrman
Designer: Don Trousdell
Illustrators: Nancy Hoefig, Sandi Glass,
    Ellen Lord, Cecil Dorman

Typesetter: Cheap Type
Color Separator: Glundal Color
Publication Printer: Lakeside Press

Title: Conoco '76
Art Director: Milt Simpson
Designer: Mary Ann Nichols
Illustrators: Jerry Stefl, Don Johnson, Mary Ann Nichols
Photographers: MacGillivray-Freeman Films, Maury Bates,
Tony Sheldon Moir, Bill Witt
Typesetter: Arrow Typographers, Inc.
Color Separator: Great Lakes Press
Publication Printer: Great Lakes Press
Paper Manufacturer: Northwest

Title: R.F. Illustrated
Art Director: Jack Beck
Typesetter: Unbikant
Publication Printer: S. D. Scott

Title: Spartan Food Systems Annual Report
Art Directors: Tom Wood, Creative Services, Inc.
Designers: Tom Wood, Creative Services, Inc.
Photographer: Arthur Tilley
Typesetter: Typography
Paper Manufacturer: Litho-Krome

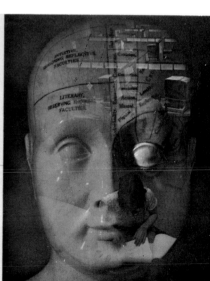

Title: Chilton Co. Annual Report
Art Director: Jim Naughton
Designer: Ed Dahl
Photographer: Jim Conroy
Typesetter: Chilton
Color Separator: Gilbert Color
Publication Printer: Chilton Printing
Paper Manufacturer: Champion

Title: Syracuse Univ. Annual Report
Art Director: Carl T. Herrman
Designer: Don Trousdell
Illustrator: Sandi Glass
Photographer: Frank Shoemaker
Typesetter: Cheap Type
Color Separator: Cojac Press
Publication Printer: Cojac Press
Paper Manufacturer: Warren

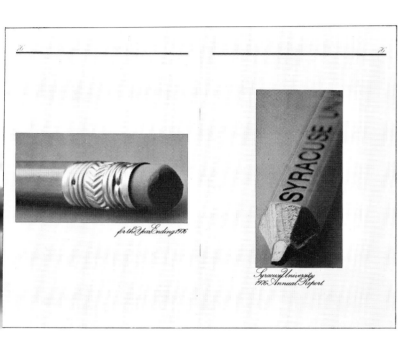

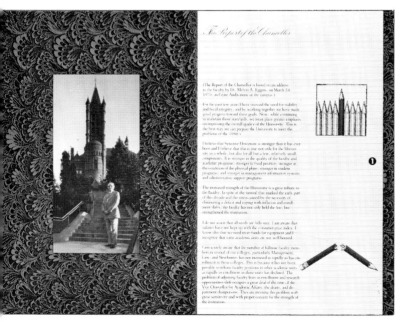

Title: Exxon Annual Report
Art Director: Harry O. Diamond
Designer: Harry O. Diamond
Illustrator: Fred Otnes
Typesetter: Tri-Arts Press, Inc.
Color Separator: The Case-Hoyt Corporation
Publication Printer: The Case-Hoyt Corporation
Paper Manufacturer: Warren Paper Co.

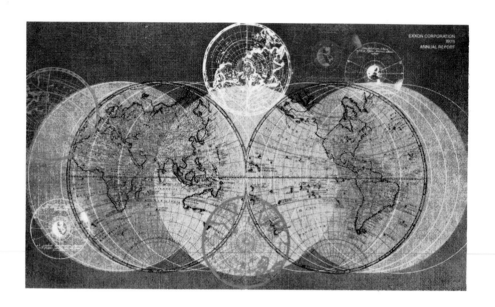

The company completed an extensive seismic survey on new concessions in the Mediterranean offshore Libya. The data are being evaluated. Onshore, seismic work continues on other acreage acquired in 1974. Production in Libya increased 4 percent over 1974 levels, and the gas plant at Brega produced at a record rate of 85,000 barrels a day of liquefied gas.

In the Far East, exploration and production operations were suspended in Malaysia pending negotiation of a satisfactory production-sharing contract with the government. Production continued in the Tembungo field offshore the state of Sabah under interim arrangements, at a rate of about 4,000 barrels a day. Construction began on two producing platforms to develop the Tuna and Mackerel fields in Australia's Bass Strait. Their production will offset declining production from older fields in this area.

The company is developing a variety of equipment designed to operate in deep waters. The Discoverer 534, built specifically to drill for Exxon, began operations off Burma under a long-term lease. Built to work in water depths up to 3,000 feet, the ship will test deep-water acreage off the west coast of Thailand in 1976. Esso Exploration has contracted for a second deepwater vessel for delivery in 1977. Another drilling vessel, a semi-submersible rig, was ordered by Exxon USA and is under construction in Japan. It will be capable of drilling in rough seas and in water depths up to 1,500 feet.

Exxon is conducting two pilot tests of new equipment in the Gulf of Mexico which could greatly extend the range of offshore producing operations—a Submerged Production System (SPS), which permits remote control of producing operations from the surface in waters too deep for platforms, and a "guyed tower" designed for use in water depths up to 2,000 feet, beyond the practical limits of conventional producing platforms. A prototype of the SPS was installed on an established field off Grand Isle, Louisiana, and three subsea wells were drilled in 1975. A one-fifth scale model of the guyed tower was installed for testing in 300 feet of water 35 miles off Grand Isle. Anchored to the bottom by twelve cables, the slender steel tower "gives" with the waves, and requires far less mass and strength than a rigid structure in comparable conditions.

Coal

A mine of Monterey Coal Company, an Exxon affiliate at Carlinville, Illinois, produced 2.9 million tons of coal, a 16 percent increase over 1974. Construction of a second underground mine in Illinois is 40 percent complete, and the project is on schedule for start-up in 1977.

An injunction issued by a U.S. Circuit Court of Appeals against the Secretary of the Interior forced The Carter Oil Company, an affiliate, to suspend development work in September on its first surface coal mine, the Rawhide mine near Gillette, Wyoming. The injunction arose from a suit by the Sierra Club which seeks to prevent the Department of the Interior from approving plans for Carter's mine and other coal mines in the region pending an extraordinary environmental impact statement covering four western states. This action was taken even though the mine will have a negligible effect on the

Abraham Ortel, better known by his Latinized name of Ortelius, drew this map of the Middle East published in 1584. Born in Antwerp in 1527, Ortelius began his career as a map salesman and colorist, and went on to produce the first modern atlas. His 1570 Theatrum Orbis Terrarum was a systematic collection of maps of all countries based on contemporary knowledge, such a collection had not been assembled since the days of Ptolemy. This map pictures the full sweep of the 16th century Turkish Empire, from the gates of Vienna to the Arabian peninsula. Place names are in Latin, with towns denoted by tiny buildings, including a surprising (and unlikely) number in the middle of the Arabian desert. Fighting ships are pictured in the Mediterranean, and what appears to be a sea monster surfaces in the Black Sea. An inscription describes the kingdom of Ormus, which paid tribute to Portugal and had its capital on an island in the Persian Gulf. According to Ortelius, the territory of Ormus, which gives its name to the modern Strait of Hormuz at the entrance of the Gulf, included the entire eastern coast of Arabia and a large section of what is now southern Iran. Altogether, the lands shown on this map possess nearly two-thirds of the world's known petroleum reserves. Exxon has major sources of crude oil in Saudi Arabia, Abu Dhabi, Qatar, Iran and Libya, and last year conducted exploration offshore Egypt, in both the Mediterranean and the Red Sea, and offshore Libya. Contrasted with the features of the map are the dramatic lines of the new University of Petroleum and Minerals in Dhahran, Saudi Arabia. In the superimposed photograph, an airliner flies over the tower which is the university's dominant feature. The four lines of Arabic are from the 1974 annual report of the Arabian American Oil Company, in which Exxon holds a 29.67 percent interest. They describe Aramco's contributions for educational and philanthropic purposes in that year, including $1,500,000 to the university

Title: Tri Quarterly 37
Art Director: Lawrence Levy
Designer: Lawrence Levy
Photographer: Michael Vollan
Typesetter: Headlineshop
Color Separator: Rohner Printing
Publication Printer: Rohner Printing

Title: Standard Brands Annual Report
Art Director: Don Weller
Designers: Don Weller, Chikako Matsubayashi
Illustrator: Don Weller
Photographer: Stan Caplan
Typesetter: Andresen Typographics
Color Separator: Anderson Litho
Publication Printer: Anderson Litho

Title: Imagination XX, Rivers U.S.A.
Art Director: Miho
Designer: Miho
Illustrators: Various
Photographers: Various
Typesetter M.J. Baumwell
Color Separator: Crafton Graphics
Publication Printer: Crafton Graphics
Paper Manufacturer: Champion Papers

Title: The Printing Salesman's Herald
Art Directors: Roger Cook, Don Shanosky
Designers: Roger Cook, Don Shanosky
Photographer: Art Kane
Typesetter: Cardinal Type Service
Color Separator: The Case-Hoyt Corp
Publication Printer: The Case-Hoyt Corp
Paper Manufacturer: Champion Papers

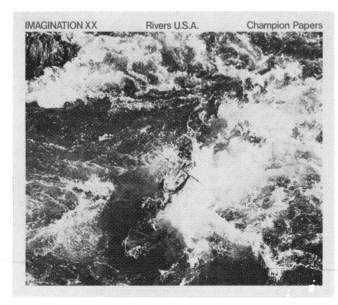

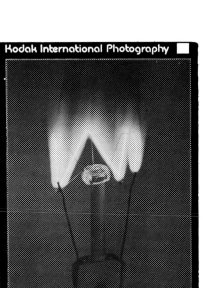

Title: Kodak International Photography
Art Directors: Kenn Jacobs, Erwin Ritenis
Designer: Erwin Ritenis
Photographer: Serge Lutens

Typesetter: Rochester Monotype Inc.
Color Separator: Rochester Polychrome Press Inc.
Printer: Rochester Polychrome Press Inc.
Paper Manufacturer: Northwest Paper Co.

Total Unit Design — Special Insert

Title: The Arthur Young Journal
Art Director: David Starwood
Designer: Will Martin
Photographers: Don Jim, Lee Boltin, Beverly Peterson
Typesetter: Boro
Printer: S. D. Scott

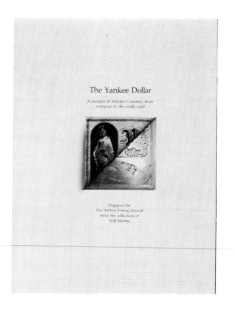

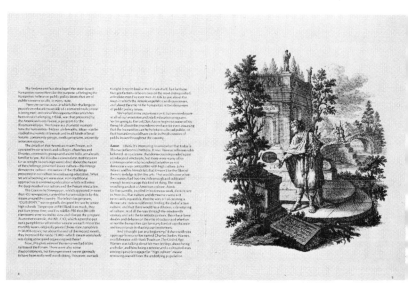

Title: Continuum
Art Director: George Bedirian
Designer: George Bedirian
Illustrator: George Bedirian
Photographer: George Bedirian
Typesetter: Rochester Typographic Service, Inc.
Color Separator: Flower City Printing
Publication Printer: Flower City Printing
Paper Manufacturer: Mead Papers

Title: Resident & Staff Physician
Art Director: Michael A. Shipman
Designer: Conrad W. Wienk
Typesetter: Johnson-Kenro Typographers
Color Separator: Post Graphics Inc.
Publication Printer: Graftek Press Inc.

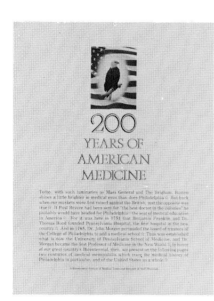

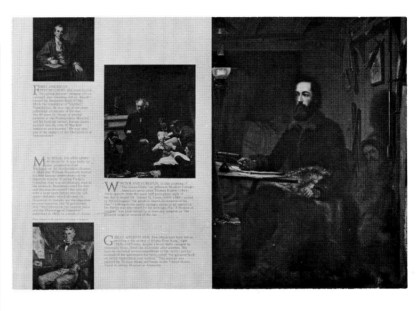

Title: Texas Monthly
Art Director: Sybil Broyles
Designer: Sybil Broyles
Photographers: Michael Patrick.
  Gary Bishop. Walter Nelson
Typesetter: G & S Typesetters
Separator: Wallace Engraving
Publication Printer: Texas Color Printer

Title: Newsweek
Art Director: Alfred Lowry
Designer: Peter Blank
Illustrator: Burt Silverman
Typesetter: Newsweek & Typographic Designers
Color Separator: Graphic Color Plate
Publication Printer: Dayton Press
Paper Manufacturer: Consolidated Papers, Inc.

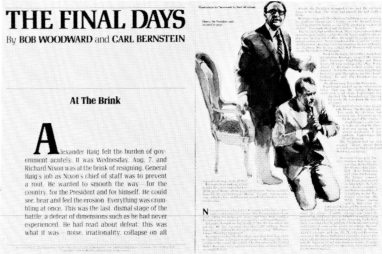

Title: Newsweek
Art Director: Alfred Lowry
Designer: Peter Blank
Illustrator: Burt Silverman
Typesetter: Newsweek & Typographic Designers
Color Separator: Graphic Color Plate
Publication Printer: Dayton Press
Paper Manufacturer: Consolidated Papers, Inc.

Title: Package Engineering
Art Director: Mary Lou Woolley
Designer: Mary Lou Woolley
Typesetter: Black Dot
Color Separator: Graftek
Publication Printer: Graftek
Paper Manufacturer: Great Northern Manufacturing Co.

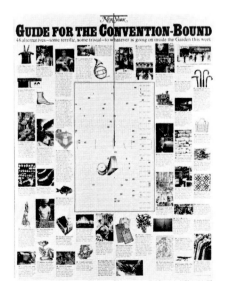

Title: New York
Art Directors: Walter Bernard, Milton Glaser
Designers: Walter Bernard, Tom Bentkowski
Illustrator: Nicholas Gaetano

Photographer: Terry Hourigan
Color Separator: Toppan/Sterling

Title: New York
Art Director: Walter Bernard
Designer: Seymour Chwast
Illustrator: Haruo Miyauchi
Color Separator: Toppan

Title: Horticulture
Art Director: Bruce McIntosh
Designer: Bruce McIntosh
Illustrators: MHS Library, Mary Purcell
Typesetter: Composing Room
Printer: R. R. Donnelley
Paper Manufacturer: Blandin

Title: Newsweek
Art Director: Alfred Lowry
Designer: Peter Blank
Photographer: Various
Typesetter: Newsweek & Typographic Designers
Color Separator: Graphic Color Plate
Publication rinter: City National; Arcata Press; & Regensteiner Press
Paper Manufacturer: Consolidated Paper Co.

Seeds, Soil and Spring Planting

THE HAPPY GARDENER.

The New Vegetable Gardener
by James Underwood Crockett

Our America

Newsweek

The most popular of all home garden plants is the tomato. We knew this, of course, when we included a free packet of tomato seeds in the February, 1974 issue. But what we never expected was the overwhelming deluge of letters from happy tomato lovers all over the country telling us how much success they had with our gift of seeds. Because we like to surprise and please our readers, we are repeating this special bonus. There are about 18 tomato seeds just right for your geographical area in the packet on this page. Each of the big, long-season plants produced from them are capable of yielding 15 to 20 pounds of luscious red fruit. All told, that's 270 to 360 pounds. Enough? If you don't plan to can or freeze all the tomatoes you can't possibly eat fresh from the garden and still warm from the sun, we suggest that you sow and grow all the seeds anyway, and give away the extra seedlings. (Two to three plants per family member will provide all the tomatoes you can use fresh, and then some.) On the back of this card is all the information you need to get started. We tell you how to sow the seeds, then pamper the seedlings, how to time your planting, and how to pinch and prune the plants to get a generous early crop of gorgeous, juice-laden tomatoes—which should weigh in at about 8 ounces each, if you have followed our growing tips carefully.

By Popular Demand

YOUR GIFT PACKET OF TOMATO SEEDS

COMPLETE DIRECTIONS FOR SUCCESSFUL TOMATO GARDENING
By JACQUELINE HERITEAU

Title: Family Circle
Art Director: John Bradford
Designer: John Bradford
Illustrator: Paul Sawyer
Photographer: Lynn St. John
Typesetter: Haber Typographers, Inc.
Color Separator: R. R. Donnelley
Printer: R. R. Donnelley

Title: Public Relations Journal
Art Director: Rudolph de Harak
Designer: Rudolph de Harak
Computer Effects: Blocpix a Division of
                    Watson-Manning, Inc.
Photographer: Carol Godshalk
Typesetter: TGI
Publication Printer: Vermont Graphics, Inc.

Title: RN Magazine
Art Directors: Albert M. Foti
Designer: JoAnne Cassella
Photographer: David Wagner
Typesetter: Arrow Typographers
Color Separator: G & S Litho
Publication Printer: Brown Printing
Paper Manufacturer: Mead Paper

Title: Communicator
Art Director: Bernard B. Sanders
Designer: David M. Seager
Illustrator: David M. Seager

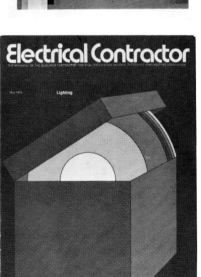

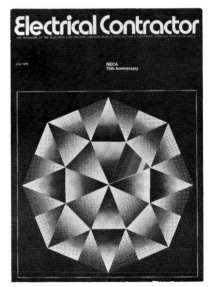

Title: Electrical Contractor
Art Director: Bernard B. Sanders
Designer: David M. Seager
Illustrator: David M. Seager

Title: Electrical Contractor
Art Director: Bernard B. Sanders
Designer: David M. Seager
Illustrator: David M. Seager

Title: Appliance Manufacturer
Illustrator: Cecil Taylor
Photographer: Black Dot
Typesetter: Direct Color
Publication Printer: Morton
Paper Manufacturer: Consolidated

Title: Institutions
Art Director: Karen Carlson
Illustrator: Bob Vuksonovich
Photographer: Type Gallery
Typesetter: Direct Color
Publication Printer: Morton
Paper Manufacturer: Consolidated Papers

Title: Southwestern Art
Art Director: Larry Smitherman
Designer: Larry Smitherman
Typesetter: Pond Typesetting
Color Separator: Wallace Engraving
Publication Printer: The Whitley Company
Paper Manufacturer: Strathmore Northwest

Title: U & lc
Art Director: Herb Lubalin
Designer: Herb Lubalin
Typesetter: LSC&P Design Group, Inc.
Publication Printer: Lincoln Graphic Arts
Paper Manufacturer: Great Northern

Title: Newsweek
Art Director: Robert Engle
Designer: Ron Meyerson
Photographer: Bill Ray
Typesetter: Typographic Designers
Color Separator: Graphic Color Plate
Publication Printer: City National Printing;
Dayton Press; & Arcata Press
Paper Manufacturer: St. Regis

Title: PSA California
Art Director: Cliff Wynne
Designer: Jeff Butler
Photographer: Jim Cornfield
Typesetter: R S Typgraphics
Color Separator: Angel Color
Publication Printer: Pacific Press
Paper Manufacturer: Crown Zellerbach

Title: Signal
Art Director: Bernard B. Sanders
Designer: David M. Seager
Illustrator: David M. Seager

Title: PSA California Magazine
Art Director: Cliff Wynne
Designer: Cliff Wynne
Photographer: Brian Leatart
Typesetter: R S Typographics
Color Separator: Angel Color
Publication Printer: Pacific Press
Paper Manufacturer: Crown Zellerbach

Title: New Engineer
Art Director: John C. Jay
Designer: Sandi Young
Illustrator: Ed Soyka
Typesetter: In House
Color Separator: Magnacolor
Publication Printer: W.A. Krueger Co.
Paper Manufacturer: Mead Papers

Title: The Real Paper
Art Director: Lynn Staley
Designer: Lynn Staley
Photographer: Bruno Joachim

Title: Sunday Plain Dealer Magazine
Art Director: Edward Freska
Designers: Nick Dankovich

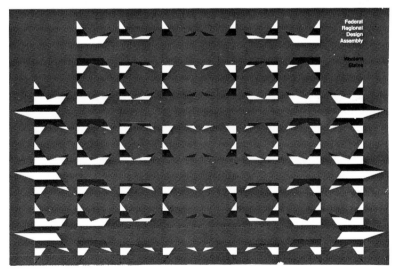

Title: Regional Design Book, 76
Art Director: James E. Johnson
Designer: James E. Johnson
Illustrator: James E. Johnson
Typesetter: Mono-Trade Co.
Publication Printer: Johnson Printing Co.

Title: MD
Art Director: Ted Bergman
Designer: Ted Bergman
Photographer: George Silk
Typesetter: Multilanguage
Color Separator: A.D. Weiss
Publication Printer: A.D. Weiss
Paper Manufacturer: S.D. Warren

Title: Modern Packaging
Art Director: Vera Finkelstein
Designer: Vera Finkelstein
Photographer: Joseph Ruskin
Typesetter: King Type
Color Separator: Brown Printing
Publication Printer: Brown Printing

Title: MD
Art Director: Ted Bergman
Designer: Ted Bergman
Illustrator: Cornelis Pietersz Bega
Typesetter: TGC & Multilanguage
Color Separator: A.D. Weiss Litho
Publication Printer: A.D. Weiss
Paper Manufacturer: S.D. Warren

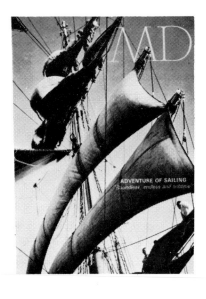

Title: The Real Paper
Art Director: Ronn Campisi
Designer: Ronn Campisi
Illustrator: Mark Fisher

Title: Modern Packaging
Art Director: Vera Finkelstein
Designer: Vera Finkelstein
Photographer: Mark Kozlowski
Typesetter: King Type
Color Separator: Brown Printing
Publication Printer: Brown Printing

Title: Medical Economics
Art Directors: Albert M. Foti
Designer: Albert M. Foti
Photographer: Bob Weir
Typesetter: Medical Economics
Color Separator: Brown Printing
Publication Printer: Brown Printing
Paper Manufacturer: Champion

Title: Medical Economics
Art Directors: Albert M. Foti
Designer: Albert M. Foti
Photographer: Bob Weir
Typesetter: Arrow Typographers
Color Separator: Brown Printing
Publication Printer: Brown
Paper Manufacturer: Champion

Title: Folio
Art Director: Victoria B. Hill
Designers: Victoria B. Hill, David G. Roussos
Illustrators: David G. Roussos, Victoria B. Hill, Vivian
Kerstein, Ardella Singleton, Jim C. Harper
Beby Evert, Q. Eddy
Publication Printer: Berger

Title: National Review
Art Director: James W. O'Bryan
Designer: James W. O'Bryan
Illustrator: James W. O'Bryan
Typesetter: Chelsea
Color Separator: Madison Engraver

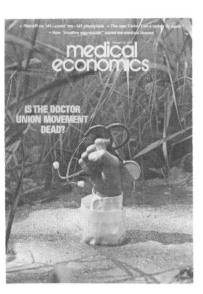

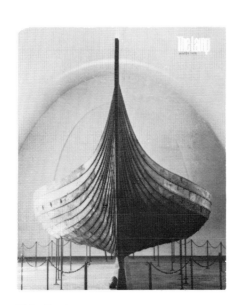

Title: FMC Progress
Art Director: Norm Bezane
Designer: Henry Robertz Design
Photographer: Manfred Ehrich
Color Separator: Regensteiner
Publication Printer: Regensteiner
Paper Manufacturer: Consolidated

Title: The Lamp
Art Director: Harry O. Diamond
Designer: Harry O. Diamond
Photographer: David Moore
Typesetter: Tri-Arts Press, Inc.
Color Separator: The Case-Hoyt Corp
Publication Printer: The Case-Hoyt Corp
Paper Manufacturer: S.D. Warren Co.

Title: The New York Times
Art Director: Eric Seidman
Designer: Eric Seidman
Typesetter: The N.Y. Times
Publication Printer: The N.Y. Times

Title: Progressive Architecture
Art Director: George W. Coderre
Photographer: David A. Morton
Publication Printer: W.A. Krueger Co.

Title: The N.Y. Times Magazine
Art Director: Ruth Ansel
Illustrator: Bill King
Typesetter: N.Y. Times
Publication Printer: The N.Y. Times

Title: The N.Y. Times/New Jersey Section
Art Directors: George Cowan, Louis Silverst[...]
Photographer: William Sauro
Typesetter: The N.Y. Times

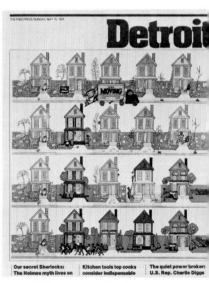

Title: Horizon, Autumn
Art Director: Ken Munowitz
Designer: Ken Munowitz
Color Separator: Chanticleer Press
Publication Printer: W.A. Krueger Co.
Paper Manufacturer: Mead Papers

Title: Home—Los Angeles Times
Art Director: Hans Albers
Designer: Alfred Beck
Illustrator: Gabor Kadar
Photographer: Phillip Cripps
Color Separator: Alco-Gravure California
Roto Gravure Division
Publication Printer: Alco-Gravure

Title: Detroit—Free Press
Designer: Roger F. Fidler
Illustrator: Harry Bartlett
Color Separator: Standard Gravure
Publication Printer: Standard Gravur[...]

Title: National Lampoon
Art Director: Peter Kleinman
Photographer: Chris Callis
Typesetter: Haber Typographers
Color Separator: Colorite
Publication Printer: Kansas Color Press

Title: MD
Art Director: Ted Bergman
Designer: Ted Bergman
Illustrator: Anonymous 18th C.
Typesetter: Multilanguage Typographers
Color Separator: A.D. Weiss Litho Co.
Publication Printer: A.D. Weiss Litho Co.
Paper Manufacturer: S.D. Warren Co.

Title: Esquire
Art Director: Michael Gross
Designers: Michael Gross, Robert Pellegrini
Photographer: Arky & Barrett
Typesetter: Cardinal Type Service
Color Separator: R. R. Donnelley
Publication Manufacturer: R. R. Donnelley

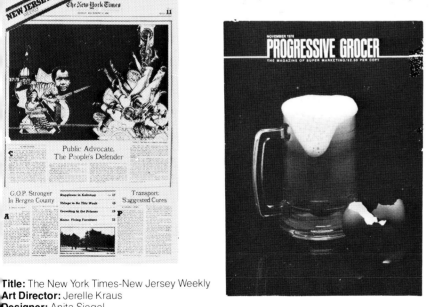

Title: The New York Times-New Jersey Weekly
Art Director: Jerelle Kraus
Designer: Anita Siegel
Typesetter: The N.Y. Times
Publication Printer: The N.Y. Times

Title: Progressive Grocer
Art Director: Robert P. Ericksen
Designer: Robert P. Ericksen
Photographer: Bruce Nemeth
Color Separator: National Bickford
Publication Printer: City National

Title: Quest 77
Art Director: Noel Werrett
Designer: Noel Werrett
Photographer: Gaston Rebuffat, Rappo
Typesetter: Cardinal Type Service
Color Separator: R. R. Donnelly
Publication Printer: R. R. Donnelly
Paper Manufacturer: Westvaco

Title: Design Quarterly
Art Director: James E. Johnson
Designer: James E. Johnson
Illustrator: James E. Johnson
Typesetter: Mono-Trade Co.
Publication Printer: Kolor-Press

Title: Tooling & Production
Art Director: E. J. Brooks
Designer: E. J. Brooks
Photographer: Ted and Shirley Black
Typesetter: PhototyPe
Color Separator: Lash Lithoplate Co.
Publication Printer: Gray Printing Co.
Paper Manufacturer: Champion Papers

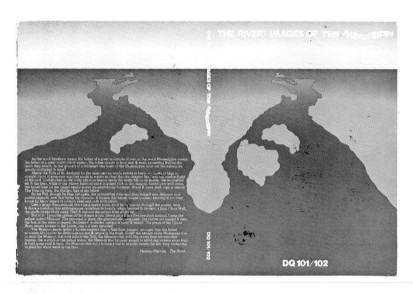

Title: Atlanta
Art Director: Suzanne S. Anderson
Designer: Art Riser
Illustrator: Reagan Wilson
Typesetter: Typography Shop
Color Separator: Lithoplates Inc.
Publication Printer: Williams

Title: Atlanta
Art Director: Suzanne S. Anderson
Designer: Suzanne S. Anderson
Illustrator: Warren Weber
Typesetter: Typography Shop
Color Separator: Lithoplates Inc.
Publication Printer: Williams

Title: Metlfax
Art Director: E. J. Brooks
Designer: E. J. Brooks
Photographer: Jack Short
Typesetter: Phototype
Color Separator: Lash Lithoplate Co.
Publication Printer: Gray Printing Co.
Paper Manufacturer: Champion Papers

Title: Executive Housekeeper
Art Director: Frank Moore
Designer: Frank Moore
Photographer: Chas. P. Mills Studio
Publication Printer: The McFarland Co

Title: RN Magazine
Art Directors: Albert M. Foti
Designer: JoAnne Cassella
Photographer: Jerry Sarapochiello
Typesetter: Arrow Typographers
Color Separator: G & S Litho
Publication Printer: Brown Printing
Paper Manufacturer: Mead Papers

Title: Executive Housekeeper
Art Director: Frank Moore
Designer: Frank Moore
Photographer: Chas. P. Mills Studio
Publication Printer: The McFarland Co

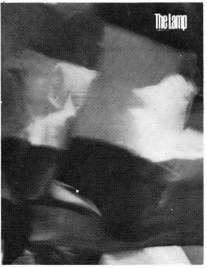

Title: The Lamp
Art Director: Harry O. Diamond
Designer: Harry O. Diamond
Photographer: Samuel Varnedoe
Typesetter: Tri-Arts Press Inc.
Color Separator: The Case-Hoyt Corp
Publication Printer: The Case-Hoyt Corp
Paper Manufacturer: S.D. Warren Co.

Title: Architectural Record
Art Director: Alex Stillano
Designer: Alex Stillano
Photographer: Ronald Livieri
Typesetter: Judd & Detweiler
Color Separator: National Colorgraphics
Publication Printer: Judd & Detweiler

Title: The Lamp
Art Director: Harry O. Diamond
Designer: Harry O. Diamond
Photographer: Co Rentmeester
Typesetter: Tri-Arts Press, Inc.
Color Separator: The Case-Hoyt Corp
Printer: The Case-Hoyt Corporation
Paper Manufacturer: Warren Paper Co.

Title: Food Distributors News
Art Director: Bernard B. Sanders
Designer: David M. Seager
Illustrator: David M. Seager

Title: The Arthur Young Journal
Art Director: David Starwood
Designer: David Starwood
Publication Printer: Johnson/Kenro, Boro

Title: Food Distributors News
Art Director: Bernard B. Sanders
Designer: David M. Seager
Illustrator: David M. Seager

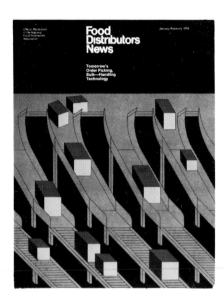

Title: Historic Preservation
Art Director: Wendy Adler
Designer: Red Truck Farm
Illustrators: Paul Hogarth, Jasper Johns
Color Separator: GraphTec
Publication Printer: The John D. Lucas Printing Company
Paper Manufacturer: Mohawk Paper Mills, Inc.

Title: American Vocational Journal
Art Director: Bernard B. Sanders
Designer: David M. Seager
Illustrator: David M. Seager

Title: American Vocational Magazine
Art Director: Bernard B. Sanders
Designer: David M. Seager
Illustrator: David M. Seager

Title: American Vocational Journal
Art Director: Bernard B. Sanders
Designer: David M. Seager
Illustrator: David M. Seager

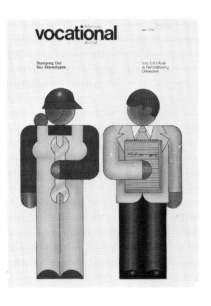

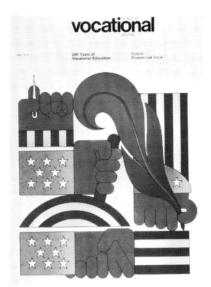

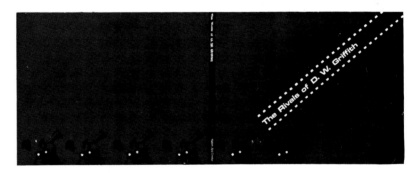

Title: American Vocational Journal
Art Director: Bernard B. Sanders
Designer: David M. Seager
Illustrator: David M. Seager

Title: The Rivals of D.W. Griffith
Art Director: James E. Johnson
Designer: Sandra K. Johnson
Illustrator: Sandra K. Johnson
Typesetter: Auto-Composition Co.
Publication Printer: North Central

Title: RN Magazine
Art Directors: Albert M. Foti. JoAnne Cassella
Designer: JoAnne Cassella
Photographer: Jerry Sarapochiello
Typesetter: Arrow Typographers
Color Separator: G & S Litho
Publication Printer: Brown Printing
Paper Manufacturer: Mead Papers

Title: RN Magazine
Art Directors: Albert M. Foti. JoAnne Cassella
Designer: JoAnne Cassella
Photographer: Steve Eisenberg
Typesetter: Arrow Typographers
Color Separator: G & S Litho
Publication Printer: Brown Printing
Paper Manufacturer: Mead Papers

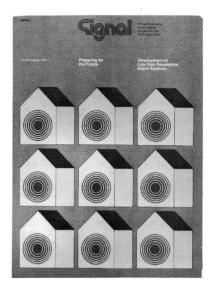

Title: Signal
Art Director: Bernard B. Sanders
Designer: David M. Seager
Illustrator: David M. Seager

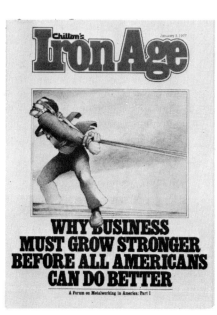

Title: IA
Art Director: Jim Naughton
Designers: Ed Dahl, Trez Cattie
Typesetter: Chilton
Color Separator: Gilbert Color
Publication Printer: Chilton Printing
Paper Manufacturer: Champion Papers

Title: Landscape Architecture
Art Directors: Dan Hobbs, Steve Hall
Designers: Dan Hobbs, Steve Hall
Illustrator: Albert Bierstadt
Typesetter: Adpro Services
Color Separator: Photo-Offset
Publication Printer: Gateway Press

Title: Pacific Business
Art Director: Patricia Davis
Designer: Patricia Davis
Photographer: Light Language
Typesetter: Ad Type
Color Separator: Cal Central Press
Publication Printer: Cal Central Press
Paper Manufacturer: S. D. Warren

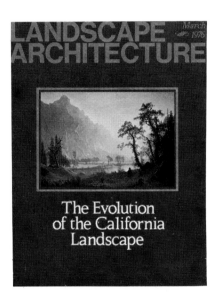

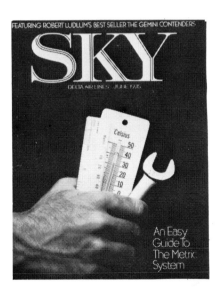

Title: Sky
Art Director: Ray Yee
Designer: Ray Yee
Photographer: Stan Caplan
Typesetter: Headliners
Color Separator: Roberts Graphic Arts
Publication Printer: Arcadia Graphics
Paper Manufacturer: Crown Zellerbach

Title: MD
Art Director: Ted Bergman
Designer: Ted Bergman
Photographer: Joel Gordon
Typesetter: Multilanguage Typographers
Color Separator: A.D. Weiss Litho Co.
Publication Printer: A.D. Weiss Litho Co.
Paper Manufacturer: S.D. Warren Co.

Page Design — Single Page

Title: Boston
Art Director: Ronn Campisi
Designer: Ronn Campisi
Illustrator: Marty Braun
Typesetter: Publishers Design & Production
Publication Printer: Chilton

Title: People
Art Director: Robert N. Essman
Photographer: Anthony K. Roberts
Typesetter: Time Inc.
Publication Printer: R.R. Donnelley

Title: Horticulture
Art Director: Bruce McIntosh
Designer: Bruce McIntosh
Illustrator: Stephanie Fleischer
Photographer: Wide World Photos
Typesetter: Composing Room
Publication Printer: R.R. Donnelley
Paper Manufacturer: Blandin Paper Co.

Title: Family Circle
Art Director: Teresa Montalvo
Designer: Chas. B. Slackman
Typesetter: Haber Typographers, Inc.
Color Separator: R.R. Donnelley
Publication Printer: R.R. Donnelley

Title: Esquire
Art Director: Michael Gross
Designer: Jane Prettyman
Typesetter: Cardinal Typographers
Color Separator: R. R. Donnelley
Publication Manufacturer: R. R. Donnelley

Title: The N.Y. Times Arts & Leisure
Section
Art Director: Nicki Kalish
Designer: Nicki Kalish
Illustrator: Oliver Williams
Photographers: Dina Makarova, Mike Wells
Typesetter: The New York Times
Publication Printer: The New York Times

Title: The Oakland Press
Art Director: David Adrien
Illustrator: Rolf Winter

Title: Lifestyle—Chicago Tribune
Art Director: Gus Hartoonian
Designer: Don Krohn
Photographer: Sally Good
Typesetter: Chicago Tribune
Color Separator: Chicago Tribune
Publication Printer: Chicago Tribune

Title: Chicago Tribune
Art Director: Gus Hartoonian
Designer: Tom Heinz
Illustrator: Tom Heinz
Typesetter: Chicago Tribune
Color Separator: Chicago Tribune
Publication Printer: Chicago Tribune

Title: Chicago Tribune
Art Director: Gus Hartoonian
Designer: Tom Heinz
Photographer: Earl Gustie
Typesetter: Chicago Tribune
Color Separator: Chicago Tribune
Publication Printer: Chicago Tribune

Title: Comment
Art Director: Michael Todd
Designer: Michael Todd
Illustrator: Tomi Ungerer
Typesetter: Michael Todd/Etc. Graphics
Publication Printer: Expedi Printing

Title: The N.Y. Times
Art Director: Steve Lawrence
Designer: Guy Fery
Photographer: The N.Y. Times
Color Separator: The N.Y. Times

Title: The Real Paper
Art Director: Lynn Staley
Designer: Lynn Staley

Title: Institutional Investor
Art Director: Chel Dong
Designer: Chel Dong
Typesetter: Lane Press
Color Separator: Lane Press
Publication Printer: Lane Press

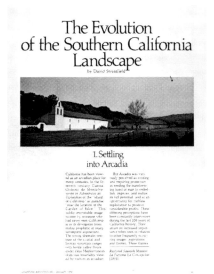

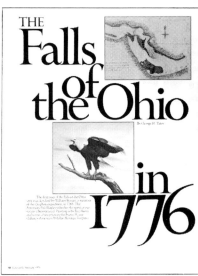

Title: Landscape Architecture
Art Directors: Dan Hobbs, Steve Hall
Designers: Dan Hobbs, Steve Hall
Photographer: David Streatfield
Typesetter: Typo/Graphic Services
Color Separator: Photo-Offset
Publication Printer: Gateway Press

Title: MD
Art Director: Ted Bergman
Designer: Ted Bergman
Photographer: Fred Fehl
Typesetter: The Universal Penman
Publication Printer: Ad. D. Weiss Litho
Paper Manufacturer: Bowater

Title: Louisville
Art Directors: Dan Hobbs, Steve Hall
Designer: Dan Hobbs
Illustrator: Ray Harm
Typesetter: Adpro Services
Color Separator: Photo-Offset
Publication Printer: Gibbs-Inman
Paper Manufacturer: Mead Paper Co.

Title: Medical Dimension
Art Director: John C. Jay
Designer: John C. Jay
Illustrator: Richard Harvey
Typesetter: In House
Publication Printer: W. A. Kreuger
Paper Manufacturer: Mead

Title: MD
Art Director: Ted Bergman
Designer: Michael Silberman
Photographer: Norman McLaren
Typesetter: Franklin Typog's. & Multilanguage
Publication Printer: A. D. Weiss Litho Co.
Paper Manufacturer: Bowater

Title: Juris Doctor
Art Director: John C. Jay
Designer: John C. Jay
Illustrator: John Cayea
Typesetter: In House
Publication Printer: W. A. Krueger
Paper Manufacturer: Mead

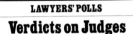

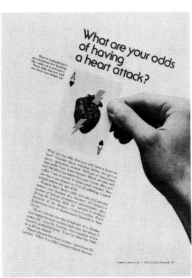

Title: Juris Doctor
Art Director: John C. Jay
Designer: John C. Jay
Illustrator: Lance Miyamoto
Typesetter: In House
Publication Printer: W. A. Krueger
Paper Manufacturer: Mead

Title: Clinical Laboratorian
Art Directors: Albert M. Foti, Thomas Phon
Designer: Thomas Phon
Photographer: Steve Eisenberg
Typesetter: Medical Economics Co.
Color Separator: G & S Litho
Publication Printer: Mack Printing
Paper Manufacturer: Mead Paper Co.

Title: Progressive Grocer
Art Director: Jeff Babitz
Designer: Jeff Babitz
Photographer: Bruce Nemeth
Typesetter: Centennial Printers
Color Separator: National Bickford
Publication Printer: City National

Page Design — Single Spread

Title: Landscape Architecture
Art Directors: Dan Hobbs, Steve Hall
Designers: Dan Hobbs, Steve Hall
Photographer: Yomiuri Shimbun
Typesetter: Adpro Services and Type Plus
Publication Printer: Gateway Press

Title: Landscape Architecture
Art Directors: Dan Hobbs, Steve Hall
Designers: Dan Hobbs, Steve Hall
Typesetter: Typo/Graphic Services and Type Plus
Publication Printer: Gateway Press

Title: McCall's
Art Director: Alvin Grossman
Designer: Alvin Grossman
Photographer: Irwin Horowitz

Title: La Business
Art Director: Bob Kinkead
Designer: Bob Kinkead
Illustrator: Glen LeCheminant

Photographer: Bill Guin
Typesetter: Lienett Co.
Publication Printer: Lienett Co.

Title: Moneysworth
Art Director: Tom Bodkin
Designer: Herb Lubalin
Illustrator: Jerome Snyder
Typesetter: Moneysworth
Publication Printer: Vineland Printing
Paper Manufacturer: Bowater Manufacturing Co.

Title: Progressive Grocer
Art Director: Jeff Babitz
Designer: Jeff Babitz
Photographer: Bruce Nemeth
Typesetter: Centennial Printers
Color Separator: National Bickford
Publication Printer: City National

Title: California Business
Art Director: Bob Kinkead
Designer: Bob Kinkead

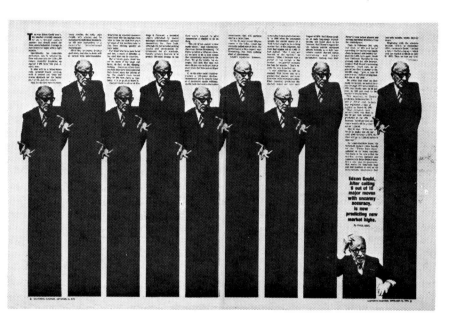

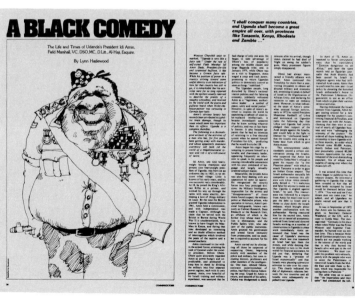

Title: Comment
Art Director: Michael Todd
Designer: Michael Todd
Illustrator: Paul Russell
Typesetter: ETC Graphics/Michael Todd
Publication Printer: Expedi Printing

Title: Sunday Magazine
Art Director: Edward Freska
Designer: Nick Dankovich
Photographer: Robert E. Dorksen
Typesetter: Art Gravure Corp. of Ohio
Color Separator: Art Gravure Corp. of Ohio
Publication Printer: Art Gravure Corp. of Ohio

Title: Sunday Magazine
Art Director: Edward Freska
Designer: Nick Dankovich
Photographer: Scott McAleer
Typesetter: Art Gravure Corp. of Ohio
Color Separator: Art Gravure Corp. of Ohio
Publication Printer: Art Gravure Corp. of Ohio

Title: Sunday News Magazine
Art Director: Robert Clive
Designer: Thomas P. Ruis
Photographer: Tom Arma

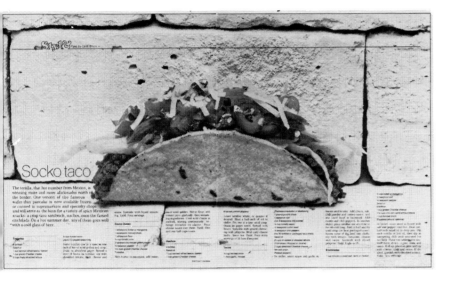

Title: Sunday Magazine   **Typesetter:** Art Gravure Corp. of Ohio
Art Director: Edward Freska   **Color Separator:** Art Gravure Corp. of Ohio
Designer: Greg Paul   **Publication Printer:** Art Gravure Corp. of Ohio

Title: Playboy
Art Director: Arthur Paul
Designers: Arthur Paul, Kerig Pope
Illustrator: Dennis Michael Magdich
Publication Printer: W. F. Hall

Title: Playboy
Art Director: Arthur Paul
Designer: Gordon Mortensen
Illustrator: Eraldo Carugati
Publication Printer: W. F. Hall

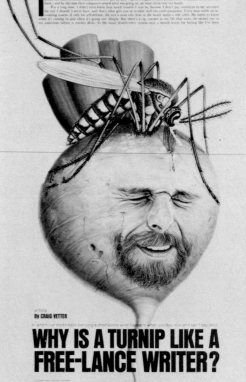

Title: Town & Country
Art Director: Ed Hamway
Designer: Brad Pallas
Photographer: Michael Tcherevkoff
Color Separator: National Bickford Graphics, Inc.
Publication Printer: Meredith Printing Corp.

Title: McCall's
Art Director: Carveth Kramer
Designer: Carveth Kramer
Photographer: Henry Wolf

Title: Texas Monthly
Art Director: Sybil Broyles
Designer: Sybil Broyles
Photographer: Bill Records

Typesetter: G & S Typesetters
Color Separator: Wallace Engraving
Publication Printer: Texas Color Printer

Title: McCall's
Art Director: Alvin Grossman
Designer: Alvin Grossman
Photographer: Henry Wolf

THE BEAUTIFUL-SKIN DIET

Title: New Times
Art Director: Steve Phillips
Designer: Steve Phillips
Photographer: Carl Fischer
Typesetter: Typros & Unitron
Color Separator: Magnacolor
Publication Printer: R. R. Donnelley

Title: New York
Art Directors: Walter Bernard, Milton Glaser
Photographer: Roberto Brosan

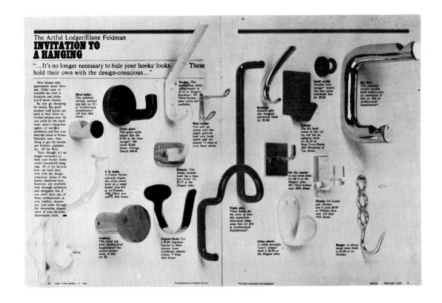

Title: McCall's
Art Director: Alvin Grossman
Designer: Alvin Grossman
Photographer: Irwin Horowitz

Title: World Tennis
Art Director: Dana S. Francis
Designer: Dana S. Francis
Typesetter: Typographic Sales Inc.
Color Separator: World Color Press
Publication Printer: World Color Press

Title: Quest/77
Art Director: Noel Werrett
Designer: B. Martin Pedersen
Illustrator: Stan Lee
Typesetter: Cardinal
Color Separator: R. R. Donnelly
Publication Printer: R. R. Donnelly
Paper Manufacturer: Westvaco

Title: Esquire
Art Director: Michael Gross
Designer: Jane Prettyman
Photographer: Steve Myers
Typesetter: Cardinal Typographers
Color Separator: R. R. Donnelley
Publication Printer: R. R. Donnelley

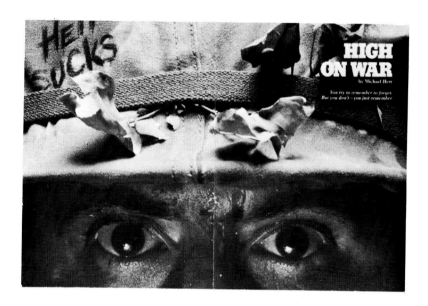

Title: Psychology Today
Art Director: Neil Shakery
Designer: Neil Shakery

Photographer: Peter Angelo Simon
Color Separator: Colins, Miller & Hutchings
Publication Printer: Meredith

Title: New Times
Art Director: Steve Phillips
Designer: Steve Phillips
Photographer: Steve Phillips
Typesetter: Typros & Unitron
Color Separator: Magnacolor
Publication Printer: R. R. Donnelley

RUNNING: THE NEW HIGH

By N.R. Kleinfield

THE ASSAULT ON ELECTRO CONVULSIVE THERAPY

by Leonard Cammer, MD

Title: Private Practice
Art Director: Charles M. Redwine
Designer: Charles M. Redwine
Photographer: David Fitzgerald
Typesetter: Ed-Be Inc.
Color Separator: The Color Separator
Publication Printer: Mid America Webpress Inc.
Paper Manufacturer: St. Regis

Title: New Times
Art Director: Steve Phillips
Designer: Steve Phillips
Illustrator: Carole Jean
Photographer: Steve Phillips
Typesetter: Typros & Unitron
Color Separator: Magnacolor
Publication Printer: R. R. Donnelly

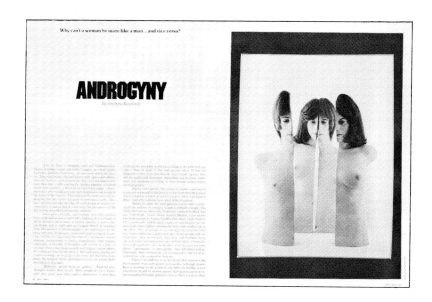

Title: Institutions
Art Director: Ron Hansen
Designer: Karen Carlson
Photographer: Dorrell Creightney
Typesetter: Type Gallery
Color Separator: Direct Color
Publication Printer: Morton
Paper Manufacturer: Consolidated

Title: McCalls
Art Director: Alvin Grossman
Designer: Alvin Grossman
Photographer: Otto Storch

Title: Perspectives
Art Director: Joseph Frassetta
Designer: Stan Timson
Illustrator: Hoedt Studio

Photographer: Frank Curcio
Typesetter: Composing Room
Publication Printer: Consolidated/Drake Press
Paper Manufacturer: Champion

Title: Kodak International Photography
Art Directors: Kenn Jacobs. Erwin Ritenis
Designer: Erwin Ritenis
Photographer: Serge Lutens
Typesetter: Rochester Monotype
Color Separator: Rochester Polychrome Press
Printer: Rochester Polychrome Press
Paper Manufacturer: Northwest Paper

Title: Package Engineering
Art Director: Mary Lou Woolley
Designer: Mary Lou Woolley
Photographer: George Zuehlke

Typesetter: Black Dot
Color Separator: Graftek
Publication Printer: Graftek
Paper Manufacturer: Consolidated

Title: Boston
Art Director: Ronn Campisi
Designer: Ronn Campisi
Illustrator: Mark Fisher
Typesetter: Publishers Design
Publication Printer: Chilton

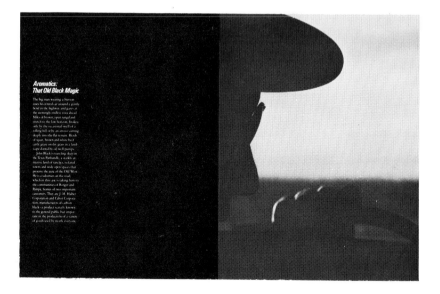

Title: Chemsphere
Art Director: John J. Conley
Designer: John J. Conley
Photographer: Bill Bridges

Typesetter: Tri-Arts Press, Inc
Color Separator: Eilert Printing
Publication Printer: Eilert Printing
Paper Manufacturer: Mohawk

Title: Kodak International Photography
Art Directors: Kenn Jacobs, Erwin Ritenis
Designer: Erwin Ritenis
Photographer: Various
Typesetter: Rochester Monotype
Color Separator: Rochester Polychrome Press
Printer: Rochester Polychrome Press
Paper Manufacturer: Northwest

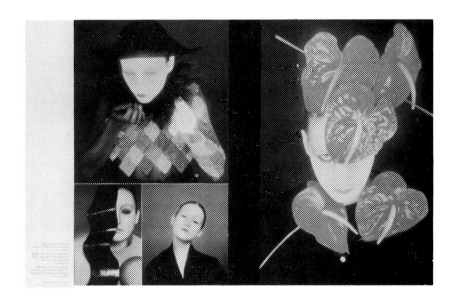

Title: Summer Times
Art Director: Carl T. Herrman
Designer: Don Trousdell
Illustrators: Nancy Hoefig, Sandi Glass, Ellen Lord, Cecil Dorman
Typesetter: Cheap Type
Color Separator: Glundal
Publication Printer: Lakeside Press

Title: Package Engineering
Art Director: Mary Lou Woolley
Designer: Mary Lou Woolley
Photographer: George Zuehlke
Typesetter: Black Dot
Color Separator: Graftek
Publication Printer: Graftek
Paper Manufacturer: Consolidated

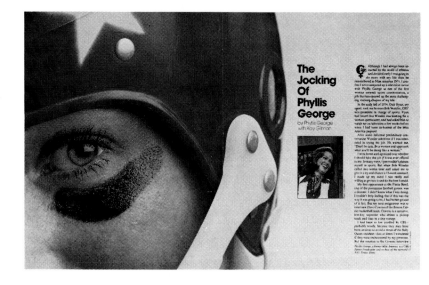

Title: Mainliner
Art Director: Chris Mossman
Designer: Chris Mossman
Photographer: Jim Cornfield
Typesetter: RS Typographics & Computer Typesetting Service
Color Separator: Lithatone
Publication Printer: Deseret
Paper Manufacturer: Crown Zellerbach

Title: Companion
Art Director: Sharon Sands-Fraser
Designer: Sharon Sands-Fraser
Photographer: Martha Swope
Typesetter: R S Typographics
Color Separator: Lithatone
Publication Printer: Holiday Press
Paper Manufacturer: Crown Zellerbach

Title: Clipper
Art Director: Sharon Sands-Fraser
Designer: Sharon Sands-Fraser
Photographer: Ron Shuman
Typesetter: Pacific Phototype
Color Separator: Roberts Graphic Arts
Publication Printer: Peninsula Lithograph
Paper Manufacturer: Crown Zellerbach

Title: Emergency Medicine
Art Directors: Ira Silberlicht, Tom Lennon
Designers: Tom Lennon, Irving J. Cohen
Photographer: Shig Ikeda
Typesetter: Allied Typographers, Inc.
Color Separator: Electronic Step and Repeat
Printer: Lincoln Graphic Arts, Inc.
Paper Manufacturer: Crown Zellerbach Corp.

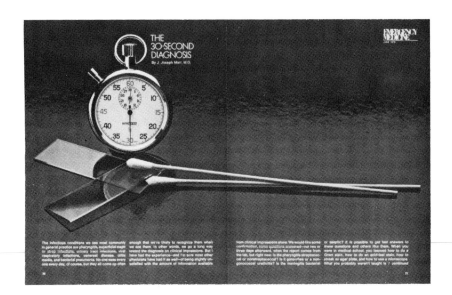

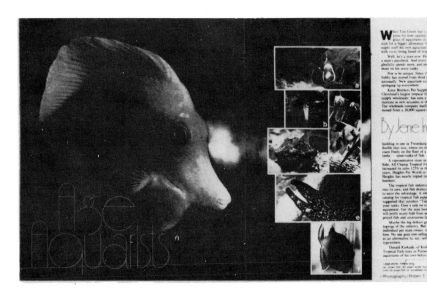

Title: Sunday Magazine
Art Director: Edward Freska
Designer: Nick Dankovich
Photographer: Robert E. Dorksen

Typesetter: Art Gravure Corp. of Ohio
Color Separator: Art Gravure Corp. of Ohio
Publication Printer: Art Gravure Corp. of Ohio

Title: Hoofbeats
Art Director: Jan V. White
Designer: Jan V. White
Photographer: George Smallsreed
Typesetter: Watkins Printing Company
Color Separator: Stevenson Photocolor
Publication Printer: Watkins Printing Co.
Paper Manufacturer: Mead Paper Co.

Title: MBA
Art Director: John C. Jay
Designer: John C. Jay
Photographer: Francis Ing
Typesetter: In House
Publication Printer: W. A. Krueger
Paper Manufacturer: Mead

Title: Interiors
Art Director: Carol Bankerd
Designer: Carol Bankerd
Photographer: Norman McGrath

Typesetter: Billboard Publications
Color Separator: Topan
Publication Printer: Billboard Publications

Title: N.Y. Times Magazine
Art Director: Ruth Ansel
Designer: Various
Photographer: N.Y. Times

Title: Texas Monthly
Art Director: Sybil Broyles
Designer: Sybil Broyles
Illustrators: Larry McEntire, Lonestar Studio

Typesetter: G & S Typesetters
Color Separator: Wallace Engraving
Publication Printer: Texas Color Printer

Title: U & lc
Art Director: Herb Lubalin
Designer: Herb Lubalin
Photographer: Alfred Gescheidt
Typesetter: M. J. Baumwell
Publication Printer: Lincoln Graphic Arts, Inc.
Paper Manufacturer: Great Northern

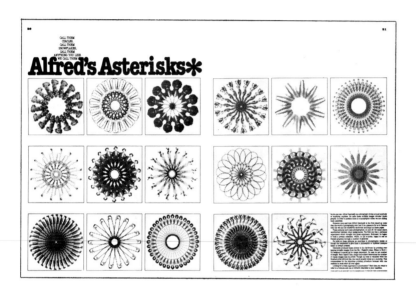

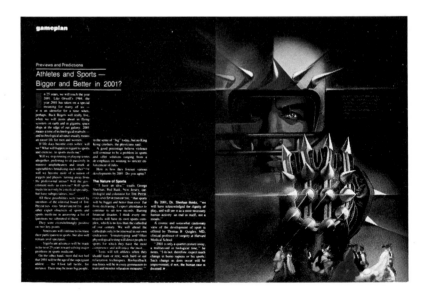

Title: Sportsmedicine
Art Director: Tina Adamek
Designer: Tina Adamek
Illustrator: Bob Peak
Typesetter: Computer Graphics
Color Separator: Andersen Graphics
Publication Printer: Hart Press

Title: Moneysworth
Art Director: Tom Bodkin
Designer: Herb Lubalin
Illustrator: Jerome Snyder
Typesetter: Moneysworth
Publication Printer: Vineland Printing
Paper Manufacturer: Bowater Manufacturing Co.

Title: Juris Doctor
Art Director: John C. Jay
Designer: John C. Jay
Illustrator: Keith Batcheller

Typesetter: In House
Publication Printer: W. A. Krueger
Paper Manufacturer: Mead

Title: Moneysworth
Art Director: Herb Lubalin
Designer: Herb Lubalin
Photographer: Tom Bodkin
Typesetter: Moneysworth Magazine
Publication Printer: Vineland Printing
Paper Manufacturer: Bowater Manufacturing Co.

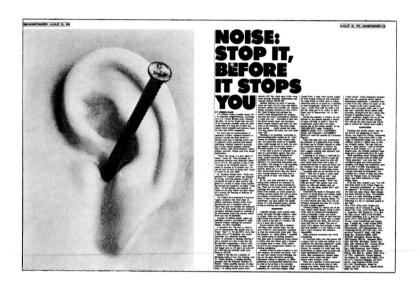

Title: Horizon
Art Director: Ken Munowitz
Designer: Ken Munowitz
Typesetter: The Composing Room
Color Separator: Chanticleer Press
Printer: W. A. Krueger Co.
Paper Manufacturer: Mead Papers

Title: The New York Times (Weekend)
Art Director: George Cowan
Designer: George Cowan
Photographer: The N.Y. Times

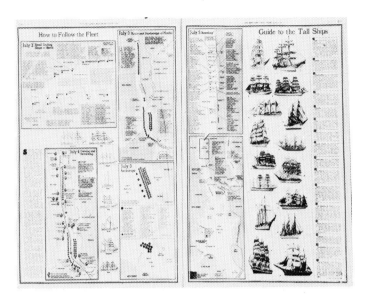

Title: U & lc
Art Director: Herb Lubalin
Designer: Herb Lubalin

Typesetter: M. J. Baumwell
Publication Printer: Lincoln Graphic Arts, Inc.
Paper Manufacturer: Great Northern

Title: Residential Interiors
Art Director: Ernest F. Costa
Typesetter: Billboard Publications, Inc.
Publication Printer: Judd & Detweiler
Paper Manufacturer: Oxford

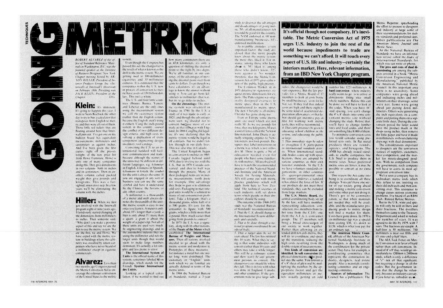

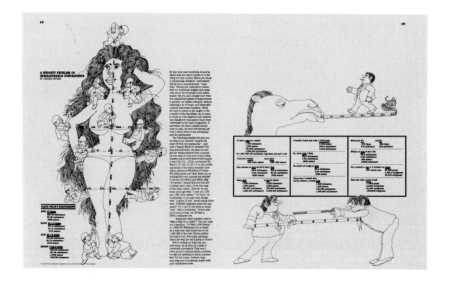

Title: U & lc
Art Director: Herb Lubalin
Designer: Herb Lubalin
Illustrator: Jerome Snyder
Typesetter: M. J. Baumwell
Publication Printer: Lincoln Graphic Arts, Inc.
Paper Manufacturer: Great Northern

Title: Esquire
Art Director: Michael Gross
Designer: Jane Prettyman
Photographer: Dick Frank

Typesetter: Cardinal Typographers
Color Separator: R. R. Donnelley & Sons
Publication Printer: R. R. Donnelley & Sons

Title: McCall's
Art Director: Alvin Grossman
Designer: Alvin Grossman
Photographer: Rudy Muller

Title: McCall's
Art Director: Modesto Torre
Designer: Modesto Torre
Photographer: George Ratkai

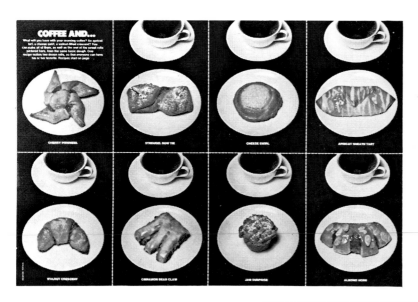

Title: People
Art Director: Robert N. Essman
Designer: Robert N. Essman
Photographer: Morgan Renard, Sygma
Typesetter: Time Inc. Videocomp
Publication Printer: R. R. Donnelley

Title: Quest/77
Art Director: Noel Werrett
Designer: Noel Werrett
Illustrator: Frank Stella (painter)
Photographer: Nancy Crampton

Typesetter: Cardinal
Color Separator: R. R. Donnelly
Publication Printer: R. R. Donnelly
Paper Manufacturer: Westvaco

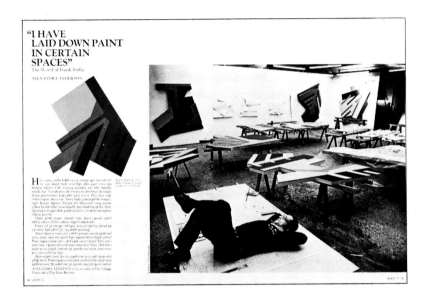

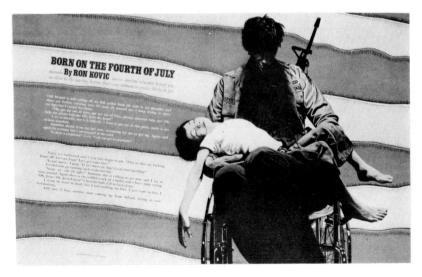

Title: Playboy
Art Director: Arthur Paul
Designer: Roy Moody

Illustrator: Greg Wray
Publication Printer: W. F. Hall

Title: McCall's
Art Director: Modesto Torre
Designer: Modesto Torre
Photographer: Henry Wolf

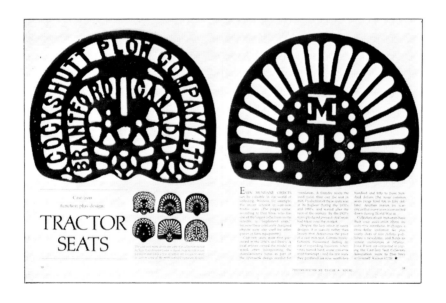

Title: Americana
Art Director: Carmile S. Zaino
Designer: Carmile S. Zaino

Typesetter: Ruttle, Shaw & Weatherill
Publication Printer: W. A. Kreuger

Title: Medical Economics
Art Directors: Albert M. Foti, William J. Kuhn
Designer: William J. Kuhn
Photographer: Bob Weir
Typesetter: Medical Economics Co.
Color Separator: Brown Printing
Publication Printer: Brown Printing
Paper Manufacturer: Blandin

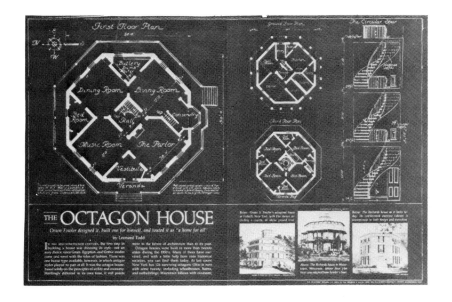

Title: Americana
Art Director: Carmile S. Zaino
Designer: Carmile S. Zaino

Typesetter: Ruttle, Shaw & Weatherill
Publication Printer: W. A. Kreuger

Title: American Heritage
Art Director: Emma Landau
Designer: Emma Landau
Photographer: Charles Phelps Cushing
Typesetter: Book Graphics Inc.
Color Separator: Chanticleer Press
Publication Printer: W. A. Krueger Co.
Paper Manufacturer: Mead Paper Co.

Title: U & lc
Art Director: Herb Lubalin
Designer: Herb Lubalin
Illustrators: Jerome Snyder, Marie Michal
Typesetter: M. J. Baumwell
Publication Printer: Lincoln Graphic Arts
Paper Manufacturer: Great Northern

Title: Review
Art Director: Chris Mossman
Designer: Chris Mossman
Photographer: Jim Cornfield
Typesetter: RS Typographic
Color Separator: Roberts Graphic Arts
Publication Printer: Donnelley Press
Paper Manufacturer: Crown Zellerbach

Title: Review
Art Director: Einar Vinje
Designer: Einar Vinje
Photographer: Jim Cornfield
Typesetter: RS Typographic
Color Separator: Roberts Graphic Arts
Publication Printer: A. D. Weiss
Paper Manufacturer: Crown Zellerbach

Title: Rolling Stone
Art Director: Roger Black
Designer: Greg Scott
Photographers: Culver Pictures, Inc., Granger Collection,
                    Bettman Archive, Jim Parcell
Typesetter: MacKenzie & Harris
Color Separator: Rolling Stone
Publication Printer: Mid-America Printing

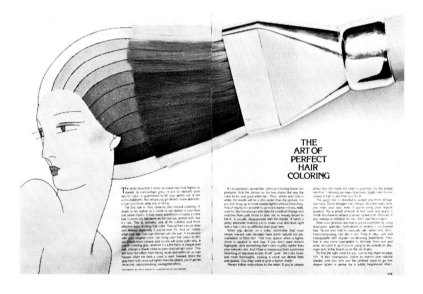

THE
ART OF
PERFECT
HAIR
COLORING

Title: McCall's
Art Director: Alvin Grossman
Designer: Carveth Kramer

Illustrator: Ron Becker
Photographer: Irwin Horowitz

Page Design — Story Presentation

Title: Town & Country
Art Director: Ed Hamway
Designer: Ed Hamway
Photographer: Douglas Kirkland
Color Separator: National Bickford
Publication Printer: Meredith Printing

Title: Review
Art Director: Einar Vinje
Designer: Lois J. Greene
Typesetter: R. S. Typographics/Headliner
Color Separator: Roberts Graphic Arts
Publication Printer: A. D. Weiss
Paper Manufacturer: Crown Zellerbach

Title: Rolling Stone
Art Director: Roger Black
Designer: Roger Black
Photographers: Stephen Shames-Photon West, Compix,
Howard Bingham, Alan Copeland-Photon
West, Black Panther Party
Typesetter: MacKenzie & Harris
Publication Printer: Mid-America Printing

Title: American Heritage
Art Director: Emma Landau
Designer: Emma Landau
Typesetter: Book Graphics Inc.
Color Separator: Chanticleer Press
Publication Printer: W. A. Krueger
Paper Manufacturer: Mead Paper

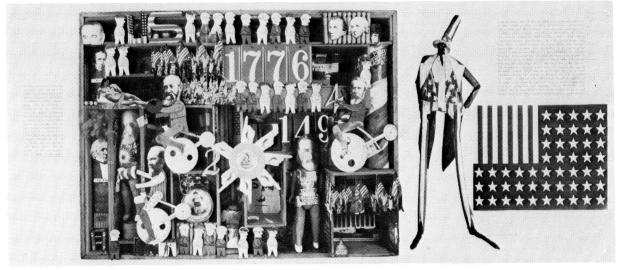

Title: Sunday Magazine
Art Director: Edward Freska
Designer: Greg Paul
Photographer: Robert E. Dorksen
Typesetter: Art Gravure Corp.
Color Separator: Art Gravure Corp.
Publication Printer: Art Gravure Corp.

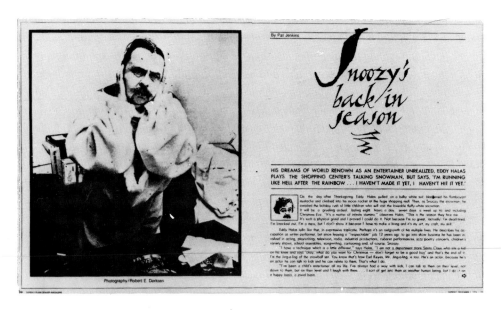

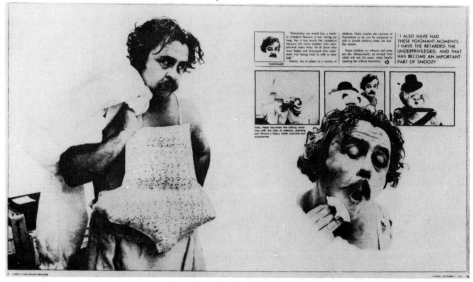

Title: Sunday News Magazine
Art Director: Robert Clive
Designer: Thomas P. Ruis
Photographer: Tom Arma
Typesetter: N.Y. News
Color Separator: N.Y. News
Publication Printer: N.Y. News

Title: The MBA Magazine
Art Director: John C. Jay
Designers: Sandi Young, Janice Warner, John C. Jay
Photographers: Francis Ing, Dennis Kugler

Typesetter: In House
Publication Printer: W. A. Kreuger
Paper Manufacturer: Mead

Title: Playboy
Art Director: Arthur Paul
Designer: Len Willis
Illustrator: Alex Ebel
Publication Printer: W. F. Hall

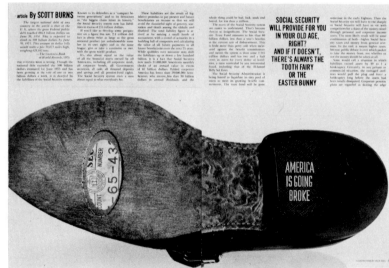

Title: Playboy
Art Director: Arthur Paul
Designer: Kerig Pope
Photographer: Bill Franz
Publication Printer: W. F. Hall

Title: Review
Art Director: Chris Mossman
Designer: Chris Mossman
Photographer: David Douglas Duncan
Typesetter: R.S. Typographics/Headliner L.A.
Color Separator: Roberts Graphic Arts
Publication Printer: R. R. Donnelley
Paper Manufacturer: Crown Zellerbach

Title: The Lamp
Art Director: Harry O. Diamond
Designer: Harry O. Diamond
Photographers: David Moore, Harry O. Diamond, Fran Diamond, Ernest Dunbar
Typesetter: Tri-Arts Press, Inc.
Color Separator: The Case-Hoyt Corporation
Publication Printer: The Case-Hoyt Corporation
Paper Manufacturer: S. D. Warren Co.

Norway's falls (opposite) yield hydroelectricity. Below: Oslo's Karl Johans gate; a Norwegian teenager; Gustav Vigeland sculpture; Edvard Munch's canal; youngsters radiate good health; Oslo apartments; detail from sail of Kon Tiki; an Esso Norway executive; Maihaugen's medieval knave; Sandefjord whaling monument; statue of Edvard Grieg

norway's new era

This already prosperous, highly industrialized country has now found oil beneath the sea. Will wealth spoil the Norwegians?

The silvery SAS jet slipped out of impossibly blue skies, lumbered down the runway at Fornebu Airport, and deposited me and a planeload of mostly Scandinavian travelers in Oslo, Norway's pleasant capital. Nestled at the head of a 60-mile-long fjord, it was a city I had previously only glimpsed from airplane windows while making brief transit stops. "Oslo is pretty quiet," my knowledgeable traveler friends had always cautioned, "don't look for any action there."

But I had come to Norway for a different kind of "action." I wanted a first-hand look at this society as booming oil activities on the Norwegian continental shelf propel this already wealthy country toward an even more prosperous future.

Last year, Norway—with four million people—enjoyed a per capita gross national product of $7,100, ranking it about $1,300 behind Switzerland and Sweden and $50 ahead of the United States. By the early 1980s, according to current estimates, Norway will displace its neighbor-rival, Sweden, as the richest industrial nation per capita in the world. Between now

by ERNEST DUNBAR

Located about a hundred miles above the Arctic Circle, the Lofoten Islands can dazzle the most jaded tourist. Rugged mountains (left) jut up dramatically from the sea to form a snowy backdrop for the midnight sun. The Lofotens are the center of a lively fishing industry and the needed important spawning grounds for cod. Below, gulls wheel over Skrova lighthouse near Svolvær.

course in engineering. I, myself, look forward to the new possibilities that all of this brings to the region."

I left the vast spaces of northern Norway to return to Oslo, where I visited with Peter Christoffersen, a young journalist and editorial writer on a Conservative newspaper. Christoffersen writes a lot about Norway's oil future these days. "What most people hope is that the government will use the oil money to reduce our taxes," he said. "We hope to get more social welfare, better hospitals, more doctors and dentists—there is still a shortage of hospital beds in Norway—and a better life for people in the isolated north.

"Among the younger generation there is also concern about the environment and the constant drive to increase the country's economic growth," Christoffersen observed. "Economic growth cannot be our only goal." He paused for a moment, reflecting on that last statement,

then added, "Of course, we have a very high standard of living and we don't want to do anything to reverse that."

After a long conversation about Norwegian politics, industrial growth and the problems that can accompany a sudden expansion in national wealth, I asked Peter Christoffersen if he was basically happy about living in Norway. "As a journalist, I've traveled all over the world," he replied without hesitation. "To the United States, South America, the Middle East, Japan and all over Europe. Norway is the only place I'd like to live."

As I left for New York, I thought of that heartfelt endorsement. I'd heard it in one form or another throughout my stay in Norway. And I began to understand why the Norwegians enjoy an international reputation as a quiet, dependable, sensible people. Somehow I don't think becoming the world's richest, industrialized country will change all that. ●

Title: Review
Art Director: Einar Vinje
Designer: Einar Vinje
Photographer: John Lewis Stage
Typesetter: B.S. Typographics/Headliner L.A.
Color Separator: Roberts Graphic Arts
Publication Printer: A. D. Weiss
Paper Manufacturer: Crown Zellerbach

Title: American Heritage
Art Director: Emma Landau
Designer: Emma Landau
Typesetter: Book Graphics Inc.
Color Separator: Chanticleer Press
Publication Printer: W. A. Krueger
Paper Manufacturer: Oxford Paper

Title: LI
Art Director: Clifford Gardiner
Publication Printer: Providence Gravure

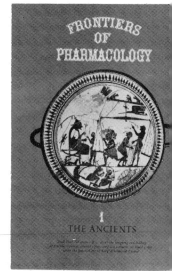

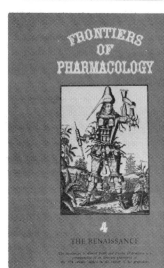

Title: MD
Art Director: Ted Bergman
Designer: Ted Bergman
Ilustrator: Misc.
Photographer: Misc.
Typesetter: Multilanguage Typographers
Publication Printer: A. D. Weiss Litho. Co.
Paper Manufacturer: Bowater

Title: American Heritage
Art Director: Emma Landau
Designer: Emma Landau
Typesetter: Book Graphics Inc.
Color Separator: Chanticleer Press
Publication Printer: W. A. Krueger
Paper Manufacturer: Oxford Paper

Title: Texas Monthly
Art Director: Sybil Broyles
Designer: Sybil Broyles
Photographers: Michael Patrick, Gary Bishop,
                    Walter Nelson
Typesetter: G & S Typesetters
Color Separator: Wallace Engraving
Publication Printer: Texas Color Printer

Title: American Heritage
Art Director: Emma Landau
Designer: Emma Landau
Photographer: Charles Phelps Cushing
Typesetter: Book Graphics Inc.
Color Separator: Chanticleer Press
Publication Printer: W. A. Krueger
Paper Manufacturer: Mead Paper

A STEP BACK IN TIME

A trip to the Ozarks in 1913
has left us a unique
record of a people by passed
by progress

Title: U & lc
Art Director: Herb Lubalin
Designer: Herb Lubalin
Illustrator: Erté
Typesetter: M. J. Baumwell
Color Separator: Pioneer Moss Reproductions
Publication Printer: Lincoln Graphic Arts, Inc.
Paper Manufacturer: Great Northern Manufacturing Co.

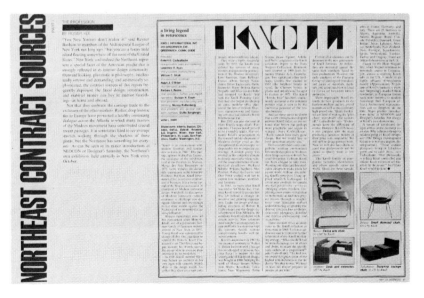

NORTHEAST CONTRACT SOURCES

Title: Residential Interiors
Art Director: Ernest F. Costa
Typesetter: Billboard Publications
Publication Printer: Judd & Detweiler

Title: New York
Art Directors: Walter Bernard, Milton Glaser
Designer: Walter Bernard
Photographer: Michael Tcherevkoff
Typesetter: Sterling
Color Separator: Toppan
Publication Printer: Arcata
Paper Manufacturer: Crown Zellerbach

Title: Medical Economics
Art Directors: Albert M. Foti, William J. Kuhn
Designer: William J. Kuhn
Photographers: Bob Weir, Stephen Munz, UPI, Wide World
Typesetter: Medical Economics Company
Color Separator: Brown Printing
Publication Printer: Brown Printing
Paper Manufacturer: Blandin Paper Co.

Title: Appliance Manufacturer
Art Director: Cecil Taylor
Photographer: C. Taylor
Typesetter: Black Dot
Color Separator: Direct Color
Publication Printer: Morton
Paper Manufacturer: Consolidated Papers, Inc.

Title: New York
Art Director: Walter Bernard
Designers: Margery Peters, Tom Bentkowski
Illustrator: Various
Photographer: Various
Typesetter: Sterling
Color Separator: Toppan
Publication Printer: Arcata
Paper Manufacturer: Crown Zellerbach

Title: U & lc
Art Director: Herb Lubalin
Designer: Herb Lubalin
Illustrator: Sam Fink
Typesetter: M. J. Baumwell
Color Separator: Pioneer Moss Reproductions
Publication Printer: Lincoln Graphic Arts, Inc.
Paper Manufacturer: Great Northern Manufacturing Co.

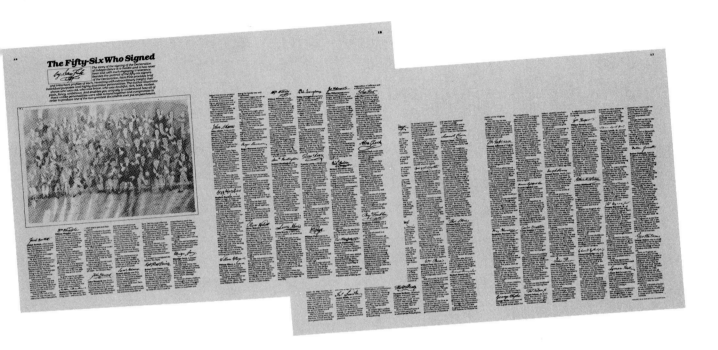

Bribery seems likely to precipitate a debate on corporate power in Congress. For the first time since the 1930s, Congress seems determined to investigate how giant corporations are managed. The image revealed by the bribery reports will be the immediate focus of the debate.

Title: MBA
Art Director: John C. Jay
Designers: John C. Jay, Frank Rothmann
Photographer: David Hedrich
Publication Printer W. A. Krueger
Paper Manufacturer: Mead

Title: Hospital Practice
Art Director: Robert S. Herald
Designer: Robert S. Herald
Illustrator: Albert Miller
Photographer: Temple University Health Sciences Center
Typesetter: Unitron Graphics Inc.
Color Separator: Nashville Electragraphics Co. Inc.
Publication Printer: R. R. Donnelly Co. Inc.
Paper Manufacturer: Consolidated Paper Co.

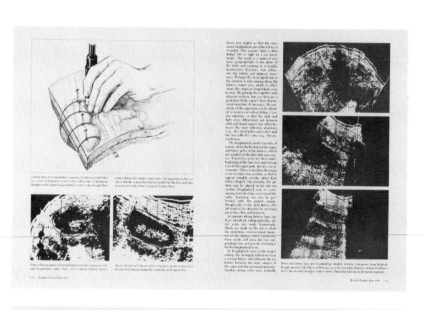

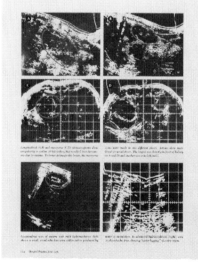

Title: Hospital Practice
Art Director: Robert S. Herald
Designer: Robert S. Herald
Illustrator: Carol Donner
Photographer: Johns-Hopkins Medical Institutions
Typesetter: Unitron Graphics, Inc.
Color Separator: Nashville Electragraphics Co.
Publication Printer: R. R. Donnelly Co., Inc.
Paper Manufacturer: Consolidated Paper Co.

Cardiovascular Nuclear Medicine: A Progress Report

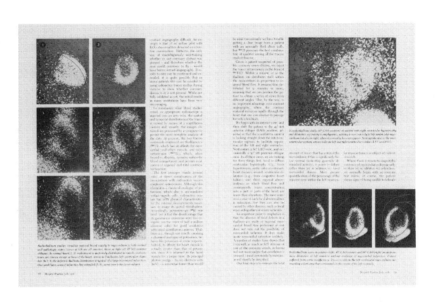

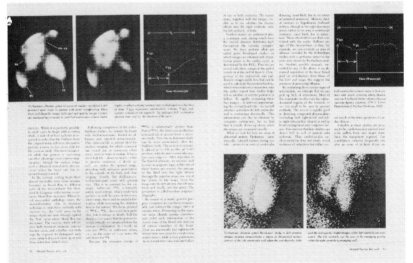

Title: National Candy Wholesaler
Art Director: Barbara Moskowitz
Designer: J. Bruce Baumann
Photographer: David Harvey
Typesetter: Byrd Pre-Press
Color Separator: Sun Crown, Inc.
Publication Printer: William Byrd Press
Paper Manufacturer: Oxford Paper

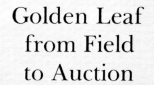

Golden Leaf from Field to Auction

Title: Hoofbeats
Art Director: Jan V. White
Designer: Jan V. White
Photographer: George Smallsreed
Typesetter: Watkins Printing Company.
Color Separator: Stevenson Photocolor Co.
Publication Printer: Watkins Printing Co.
Paper Manufacturer: Mead Paper Co.

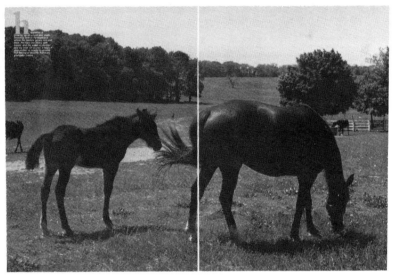

Title: Oui
Art Director: Don Menell
Designer: Don Menell
Photographer: Richard Izui
Publication Printer: World Color Press

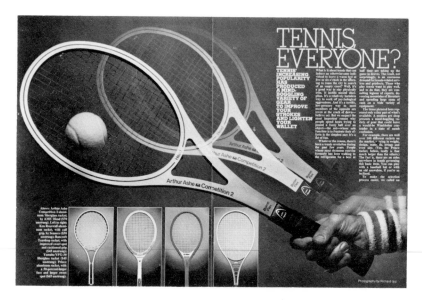

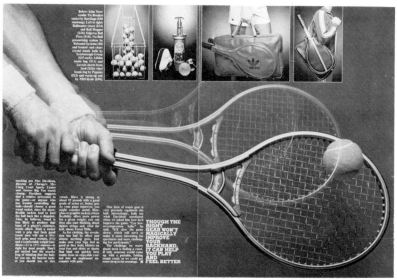

Title: Town & Country
Art Director: Linda Stillman
Designer: Brad Pallas
Photographer: Silano
Printer: Meredith Printing Corp.

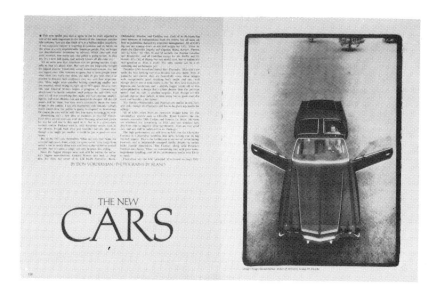

Title: Horticulture
Art Director: Bruce McIntosh
Designer: Bruce McIntosh
Photographers: Gary Taber, Bohdan Hyrnewych
Typesetter: Publishers' Design and Production Services
Color Separator: Andy Mowbray Inc.
Publication Printer: R. R. Donnelley
Paper Manufacturer: Blandin

Title: Horticulture
Art Director: Bruce McIntosh
Designer: Bruce McIntosh
Photographers: John A. Lynch, Bohdan Hrynewych
Typesetter: Composing Room
Publication Printer: R. R. Donnelley
Paper Manufacturer: Blandin

Title: U & lc
Art Director: Herb Lubalin
Designer: Herb Lubalin
Illustrator: Jerome Snyder
Typesetter: M. J. Baumwell
Publication Printer: Lincoln Graphic Arts, Inc.
Paper Maufacturer: Great Northern Manufacturing Co.

Title: Sunday Magazine
Art Director: Edward Freska
Designer: Nick Dankovich
Photographer: Ansel Adams
Typesetter: Art Gravure Corp.
Color Separator: Art Gravure Corp.
Publication Printer: Art Gravure Corp.

Title: National Candy Wholesaler
Art Director: Barbara Moskowitz
Designer: J. Bruce Baumann
Photographer: several press photographers
Typesetter: Byrd Pre-Press
Publication Printer: William Byrd Press
Paper Manufacturer: Oxford Paper

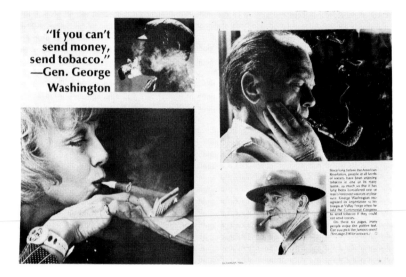

Title: National Candy Wholesaler
Art Director: Barbara Moskowitz
Designer: J. Bruce Baumann
Photographer: J. Bruce Baumann
Typesetter: Byrd Pre-Press
Publication Printer: William Byrd Press
Paper Manufacturer: Oxford Paper

Sweet Memories of the Past Are In Lititz Today

At the front of the Wilbur Chocolate Company factory in Lititz, Pa., Penny Howard, wife of company president, John Howard, sat gathered sweet remembrances of days gone by, mixed them well with the flavor and color of memories at the turn of the century, and packaged the finished product in nostalgia. The result is the Candy Americana Museum, where visitors get a short trip into the recent past, as well as an education on the present-day candies used in the manufacture of sweets that these precious made daily in the Wilbur plant at the corner of Broad Street.

Although memory methods have been updated dramatically from the type shown at right, Wilbur still makes presently, coating punchers, as well as chocolate and compound coatings, white and pastel coatings, ice cream flavor, and chocolate and compound cookie chips used for finished product manufacturers. The 50 million pounds of chocolate products which come out of the Lititz factory bears sweet, however, plus include such finished products as Vassil la, Milk and Mint Buds and Wilbur candy tops.

It all began in the 1880s when H.O. Wilbur a hard-core dealer in Vineland, N.J., went into partnership with Samuel Croft in Philadelphia to make molasses and hard candies to be sold for train boys for the railroads.

One company in Philadelphia donated several hand-operated machines which are now on display in the museum. Shown on these pages, these machines were used to shape and coil hand candies into a variety of sizes and forms. The machine at bottom left, for example, was used to turn ribbon candies which are still quite popular today during the Christmas holiday season.

Displayed on shelves behind the machines are row after row of the sturdy and colorful tin containers in which candy and some candies were sold before cardboard rescue finished the packaging industry.

In addition to serving as shipping and storage containers, these decorated tin boxes had other utilitarian advantages. Their importance at times was that they protected the manufacturers with an inexpensive way of advertising his products to the consumer and the retailer. Because the containers were discarded so often, they were often reused for other purposes after they had been emptied of candy and therefore continued to serve as reminders of the product that had originally contained, as well as a source of providing present-day Americans with vivid remembrances of the past.

Beech-Nut Gum

Here's MY kind!
Will Rogers

Title: Iron Age
Art Director: Jim Naughton
Designer: Trez Cattie
Illustrators: Ed Feldman, John Freas, Bob Knight
Typesetter: Chilton
Color Separator: Gilbert Color
Publication Printer: Chilton Printing
Paper Manufacturer: Champion

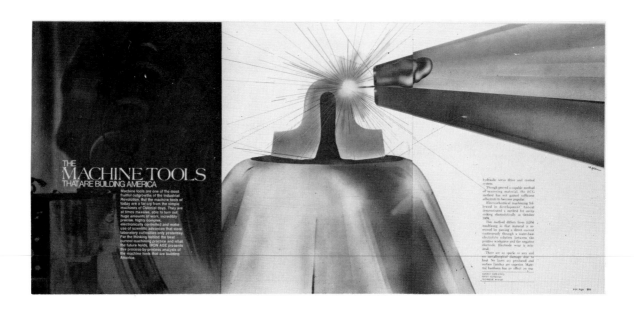

Title: Town & Country
Art Director: Ed Hamway
Designer: Linda Stillman
Photographer: Arnold Newman
Color Separator: National Bickford Graphics
Publication Printer: Meredith Printing Corp.

Title: Boston
Art Director: Ronn Campisi
Designer: Ronn Campisi
Illustrators: Mark Fisher, Mary Braun, Stephen Zinkus,
          Jim Kingston, Jon McIntosh, Amy Koch
Photographer: Bruno Joachim, John Crall
Typesetter: Publishers Design & Production Service
Publication Printer: Chilton

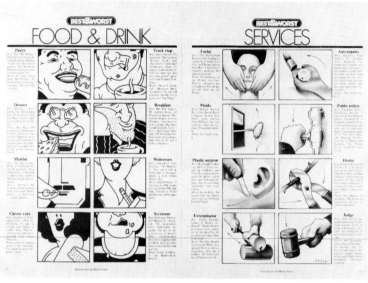

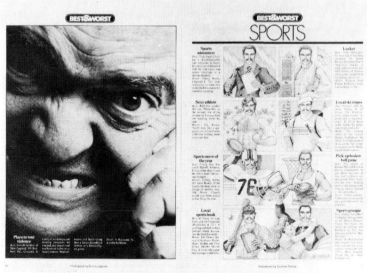

Title: MD
Art Director: Ted Bergman
Designer: Ted Bergman
Photographer: Misc.
Typesetter: Multilanguage Typographers
Color Separator: A. D. Weiss Litho Co.
Publication Printer: A. D. Weiss Litho Co.
Paper Manufacturer: Bowater

Title: U & lc
Art Director: Herb Lubalin
Designer: Herb Lubalin
Illustrator Sam Fink
Typesetter: M. J. Baumwell
Color Separator: Pioneer Moss Reproductions
Publication Printer: Lincoln Graphic Arts, Inc.
Paper Manufacturer: Great Northern Manufacturing Co.

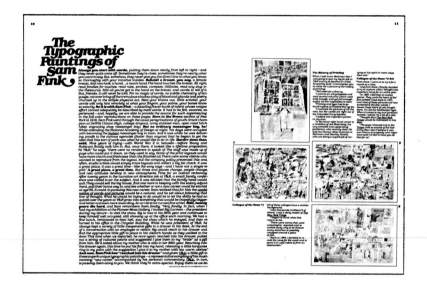

Title: U & lc
Art Director: Herb Lubalin
Designer: Herb Lubalin
Illustrator: Jerome Snyder
Typesetter: M. J. Baumwell
Printer: Lincoln Graphic Arts, Inc.
Paper Manufacturer: Great Northern

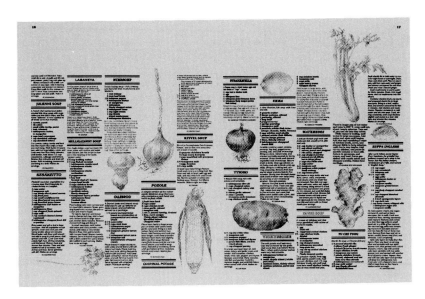

Title: U & lc
Art Director: Herb Lubalin
Designer: Herb Lubalin
Illustrator: John Alcorn
Typesetter: M. J. Baumwell
Publication Printer: Lincoln Graphics Arts, Inc.
Paper Manufacturer: Great Northern Manufacturing Co.

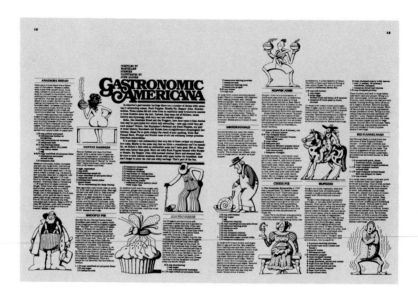

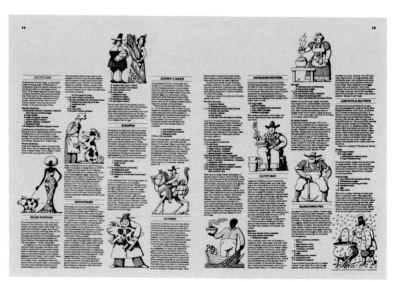

Title: U & lc
Art Director: Herb Lubalin
Designer: Herb Lubalin
Illustrator: Geoffrey Moss
Typesetter: M. J. Baumwell
Publication Printer: Lincoln Graphic Arts, Inc.
Paper Manufacturer: Great Northern Manufacturing Co.

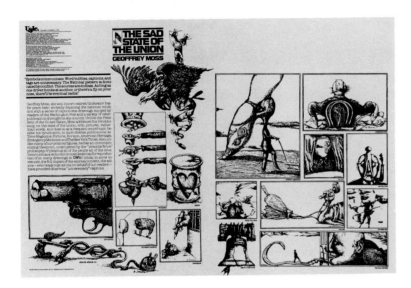

Title: Oui
Art Director: Don Menell
Designer: Don Menell
Photographer: Richard Fegley
Publication Printer: World Color Press

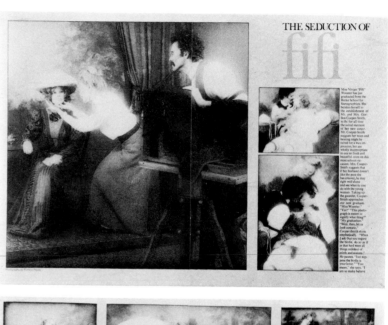

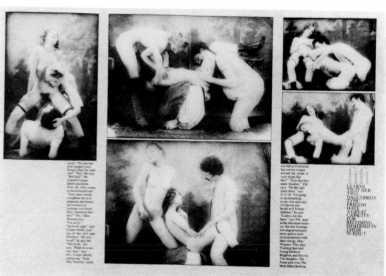

Title: McCall's
Art Director: Alvin Grossman
Designer: Hinrichs Design Associates

Title: Oui
Art Director: Don Menell
Designer: Jean-Pierre Holley
Photographer: Suze
Publication Printer: World Color Press

Title: McCall's
Art Director: Alvin Grossman
Designer: Alvin Grossman
Photographer: Otto Storch

Title: Horticulture
Art Director: Bruce McIntosh
Designer: Bruce McIntosh
Photographer: Andreas Feininger
Typesetter: Publishers' Design and Production Services
Publication Printer: R. R. Donnelley
Paper Manufacturer: Blandin

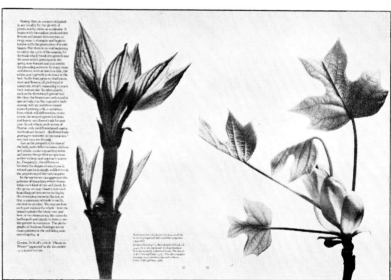

Title: Emergency Medicine
Art Directors: Ira Silberlicht, Tom Lennon
Designer: Tom Lennon
Illustrator: Oni
Photographer: Phil Gottheil
Typesetter: Allied Typographers Inc.
Color Separator: Electronic Step and Repeat
Publication Printer: Perry Printing Corp.
Paper Manufacturer: Crown Zellerbach Corp.

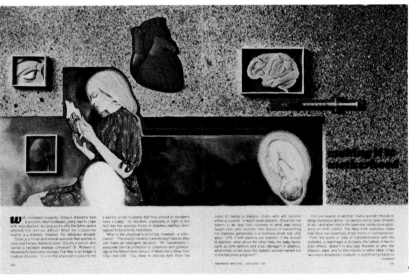

Title: Spectator
Art Director: Virg Mantle
Designers: Virg Mantle, Ruth Bridger
Typesetter: Modern Typesetting Company
Color Separator: Colorific Litho, Inc.
Publication Printer: Trio Printing Company
Paper Manufacturer: Consolidated Papers

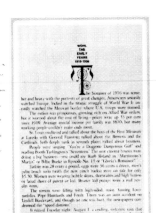

Title: Progressive Architecture
Art Director: George W. Coderre
Publication Printer W. A. Krueger

Polaroid employee photography at Kennedy Gallery

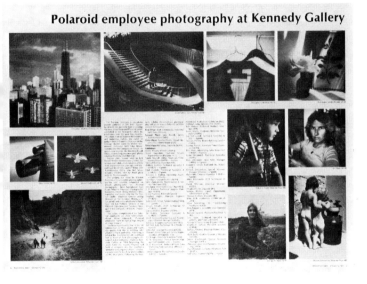

More employee photos . . .

Tigerman

Private residence, Chicago suburb

Tigerman

Title: Rolling Stone
Art Director: Roger Black
Designer: Greg Scott
Photographers: Culver Pictures, Inc., Granger Collection,
        Bettman Archive, Jim Parcell
Typesetter: MacKenzie & Harris
Color Separator: Rolling Stone
Publication Printer: Mid-America Printing

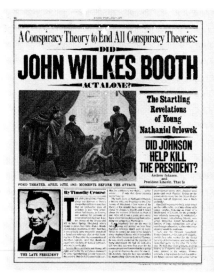
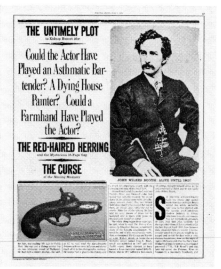

Title: Medical Economics
Art Directors: Albert M. Foti, William J. Kuhn
Designer: William J. Kuhn
Photographers: Dave Falconer, Black Star
Typesetter: Medical Economics Company
Color Separator: Brown Printing Co.
Publication Printer: Brown Printing Co.
Paper Manufacturer: Blandin Paper Co.

Title: Texas Monthly
Art Director: Sybil Broyles
Designer: Sybil Broyles
Photographer: Michael Patrick
Typesetter: G & S Typesetter
Color Separator: Wallace Engraving
Publication Printer: Texas Color Printer,

WEIRDO PAPER PLAGUES S.A.

by Griffin Smith, jr.

What's black and white and red all over? The San Antonio News—and some folks in town don't find the joke very funny.

Illustration — Cover

Title: Horticulture
Art Director: Bruce McIntosh
Designer: Bruce McIntosh
Illustrator: Robert Osborn
Typesetter: Publishers' Design and Production Services
Color Separator: Andy Mowbray Inc.
Publication Printer: R. R. Donnelley
Paper Manufacturer: Blandin Paper Co.

Title: Junior Scholastic
Art Director: Dale Moye
Designer: Jeff Derecki
Illustrator: Robert Pryor

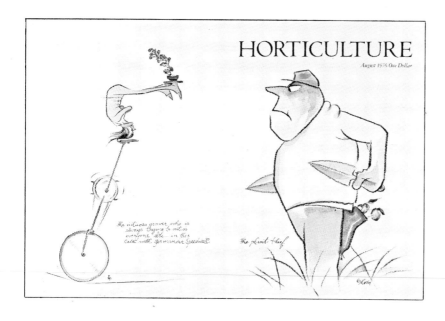

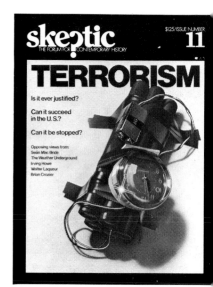

Title: The New York Times Magazine
Art Director: Ruth Ansel
Designer: Ruth Ansel
Illustrator: Seymour Chwast
Typesetter: The N.Y. Times
Color Separator: The N.Y. Times

Title: DQ Magazine
Art Director: Don S. Markofski
Designer: Don S. Markofski
Illustrator: Eric Peterson
Typesetter: VIA Type
Color Separator: Standard Graphics Arts
Publication Printer: Penn Lithographics

Title: Geriatrics
Art Directors: Phillip Dykstra, W. Bloedow
Illustrator: Jim Campbell
Typesetter: Computer Graphics, Inc.
Color Separator: Colorhouse Inc.
Publication Printer: Hart Press
Paper Manufacturer: Westvaco

Title: Geriatrics
Art Directors: Phillip Dykstra, W. Bloedow
Illustrator: Dickran Paulian
Typesetter: Computer-Graphics Inc.
Color Separator: Colorhouse Inc.
Publication Printer: Hart Press
Paper Manufacturer: Westvaco

Title: Geriatrics
Art Directors: Phillip Dykstra, W. Bloedow
Illustrator: Alex Ebel
Typesetter: Computer Graphics, Inc.
Color Separator: Colorhouse Inc.
Publication Printer: Hart Press
Paper Manufacturer: Westvaco

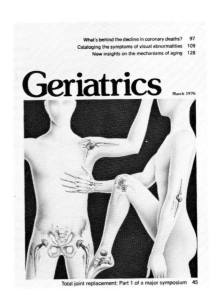

Title: Inland Printer
Art Director: Richard H. Green
Designer: Scussel-Miller Graphic Direction
Illustrator: Frank Schmandel
Typesetter: Frederick Ryder Company
Color Separator: Quasar Graphics
Publication Printer: Hart Press
Paper Manufacturer: Consolidated Papers

Title: New York
Art Director: Walter Bernard
Designer: Walter Bernard
Illustrator: Robert Grossman

Title: New York
Art Directors: Walter Bernard, Milton Glaser
Designer: Walter Bernard

Title: Arthur Young Journal
Art Director: David Starwood
Designer: David Starwood
Illustrator: Al Pisano
Photographer: Jeff Smith
Publication Printer: S.D. Scott

Title: Rolling Stone
Art Director: Roger Black
Designer: Greg Scott
Illustrator: Daniel Maffia
Typesetter: Mackenzie & Harris
Color Separator: Rolling Stone
Publication Printer: Mid America Printing

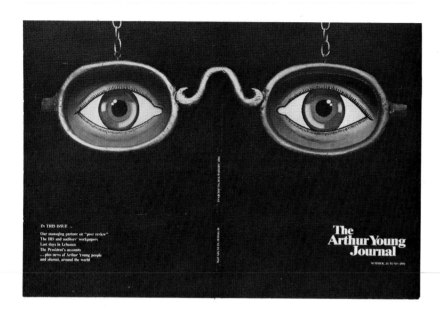

Title: L.I.-Newsday Magazine
Art Director: Clifford Gardiner
Illustrator: Gerry Gersten
Publication Printer: Providence Gravure

Title: Laboratorian
Art Directors: Albert M Foti, Thomas Phon
Designer: Thomas Phon
Illustrator: Gerry Gersten
Typesetter. Medical Economics Co.
Color Separator: G & S Litho
Publication Printer: Mack Printing
Paper Manufacturer: Mead Papers

Title: American Journal of Nursing
Art Director: Forbes Linkhorn
Designer: Forbes Linkhorn
Illustrator: Mara McAfee
Color Separator: Nashville Electrographics
Publication Printer: Rumford Press

Title: The New York Times Magazine Section
Art Director: Ruth Ansel
Designers: Roger Law, Peter Fluck
Photographer; John Lawrence-Jones
Typesetter: The N.Y. Times
Color Separator: The N.Y. Times

Title: Forbes Magazine
Art Director: Ed Wergeles
Designer: Roger Zapke
Illustrator: Larry Noble
Typesetter: Franklin Typographers
Color Separator: Collier
Publication Printer: Dayton Press
Paper Manufacturer: Mead Papers

Title: Newsweek
Art Director: Robert Engle
Designer: Ron Meyerson
Illustrator: Robert Grossman
Typesetter: Typographic Designers
Color Separator: Graphic Color Plate
Publication Printer: City National Printing
Dayton Press; & Arcata Press
Paper Manufacturer: St. Regis

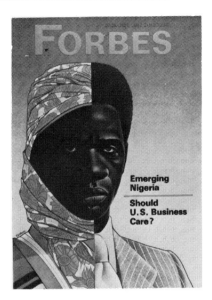

Title: Scholastic Science World
Art Director: Jeannie Friedman
Designer: Richard Brown

Title: Electronics Magazine
Art Director: Fred Sklenar
Designer: Fred Sklenar
Illustrator: Tom Upshur
Typesetter: Haber Typographers Inc.
Color Separator: Intelligencer Inc.
Publication Printer: Intelligencer Inc.

Title: The N.Y. Times School Weekly
Art Director: Joseph Sinclair
Designer: Murray Tinkelman

Title: New York News Magazine
Art Director: Robert Clive
Designer: Robert Clive
Illustrator: Bruce Stark
Typesetter: New York News
Color Separator: New York News
Printer: New York News

Title: Mainliner
Art Director: Chris Mossman
Designer: Don Weller
Illustrator: Don Weller
Typesetter: RS Typographics
Color Separator: Lithatone
Publication Printer: Deseret
Paper Manufacturer: Zellerbach

Title: Teacher Magazine
Art Director: Vincent Ceci
Designers: Vincent Ceci, Joan Hall
Illustrator: Joan Hall
Photographer: Ede Rothaus
Typesetter: Rumford Press
Color Separator: O'Brien Photoengraving
Publication Printer: Rumford Press
Paper Manufacturer: Westvaco

Title: Wood and Wood Products
Art Director: Burton Winick
Designer: Chuck Hamrick
Illustrator: Chuck Hamrick
Photographer: Roger Micus
Typesetter: Davidson Typesetting Co.
Color Separator: Central Photoengraving Co.
Publication Printer: Wayside Press

Title: Emergency Medicine
Art Directors: Ira Silberlicht, Tom Lennon
Designer: Tom Lennon
Illustrator: Richard Krepel
Typesetter: Allied Typographers, Inc.
Color Separator: Electronic Step and Repeat
Publication Printer: Lincoln Graphic Arts, Inc.
Paper Manufacturer: Crown Zellerbach

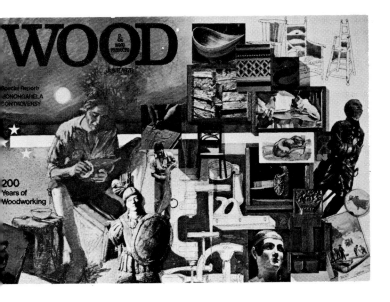

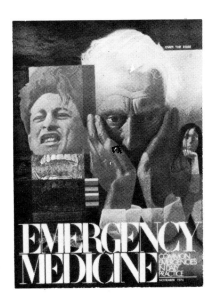

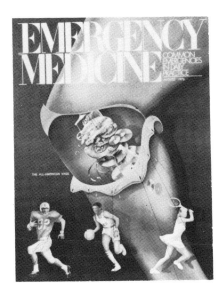

Title: Emergency Medicine
Art Directors: Ira Silberlicht, Tom Lennon
Designer: Tom Lennon
Illustrator: Judith Jampel
Photographer: Eugenia Louis
Typesetter: Allied Typographers, Inc.
Color Separator: Electronic Step and Repeat
Printer: Perry Printing Corp.
Paper Manufacturer: Crown Zellerbach Corp

Title: Emergency Medicine
Art Directors: Ira Silberlicht, Tom Lennon
Designer: Tom Lennon
Illustrator: Dickran Palulian
Typesetter: Allied Typographers Inc.
Color Separator: Electronic Step Repeat
Publication Printer: Perry Printing Corp.
Paper Manufacturer: Crown Zellerbach

Title: Emergency Medicine
Art Directors: Ira Silberlicht, Tom Lennon
Designer: Tom Lennon
Illustrator: Richard Spark
Typesetter: Allied Typographers Inc.
Color Separator: Electronic Step Repeat
Publication Printer: Perry Printing Corp.
Paper Manufacturer: Crown Zellerbach

191

Illustration — Single Page

Title: Playboy
Art Director: Arthur Paul
Designer: Norman Schaefer
Illustrator: Alex Ebel
Publication Printer: W. F. Hall

Title: Nursing 76
Art Director: John Isely
Designer: John Isely
Illustrator: Dick Oden
Typesetter: In House
Color Separator: Litho Prep
Publication Printer: Brown
Paper Manufacturer: S. D. Warren Co.

Title: Oui
Art Director: Don Menell
Designer: Rodney Williams
Illustrator: Eraldo Carugati
Publication Printer: World Color Press

Title: Boston
Art Director: Ronn Campisi
Designer: Ronn Campisi
Illustrator: Ronn Campisi
Typesetter: Publisher's Design & Production Service
Publication Printer: Chilton

Title: Oui
Art Director: Don Menell
Designer: Jean-Pierre Holley
Illustrator: Robert Grossman
Publication Printer: World Color Press

Title: The N.Y. Times
Art Director: Steve Heller
Illustrators: Roger Brown, Phyllis Kind
Typesetter: The N.Y. Times
Publication Printer: The N.Y. Times

Title: The N.Y. Times
Art Director: Steve Heller
Illustrator: Fritz Eichenberg
Typesetter: The N.Y. Times
Publication Printer: The N.Y. Times

Title: Psychology Today
Art Director: Neil Shakery
Designer: Noel Werrett
Illustrator: Alan E. Cober
Color Separator: Collins, Miller & Hutchings
Publication Printer: Meredith

Title: American Heritage
Art Director: Emma Landau
Designer: Emma Landau
Illustrator: Richard Hess
Typesetter: Book Graphics Inc.
Color Separator: Chanticleer Press
Publication Printer: W. A. Krueger Co.
Paper Manufacturer: Oxford Paper Co.

Title: Rolling Stone
Art Director: Roger Black
Designer: Greg Scott
Illustrator: Robert Grossman
Typesetter: Mackenzie & Harris
Color Separator: Rolling Stone
Publication Printer: Mid-America Printing

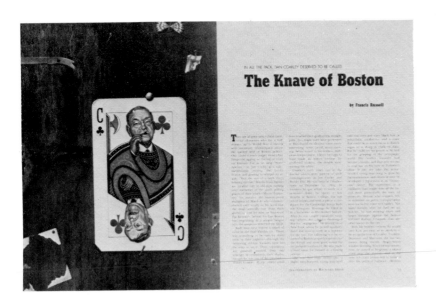

Title: The N.Y. Times
Art Director: Steve Heller
Illustrator: Ernest Aebi
Typesetter: The N.Y. Times
Publication Printer: The N.Y. Times

Title: The N.Y. Times
Art Director: Steve Heller
Illustrator: Brad Holland
Typesetter: The N.Y. Times
Publication Printer: The N.Y. Times

Title: The N.Y. Times
Art Director: Steve Heller
Illustrator: Ralph Steadman
Typesetter: The N.Y. Times
Publication Printer: The N.Y. Times

Title: The Arthur Young Journal
Art Director: David Starwood
Designer: David Starwood
Illustrator: Loretta Trezzo
Typesetter: Johnson & Kenro, Boro
Publication Printer: S. D. Scott

Title: Psychology Today
Art Director: Neil Shakery
Designer: Neil Shakery
Illustrator: James Grashow
Publication Printer: Meredith

THE PRESIDENT'S ACCOUNTS

The Rich Rewards of REWARDS

by Alan E. Kazdin

Title: L.I.-Newsday Magazine
Illustrator: Bob Newman
Publication Printer: Providence Gravure

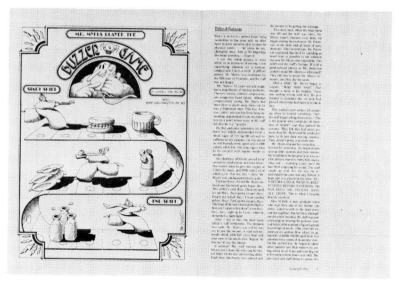

Title: Nursing 76
Art Director: Matie Anne Patterson
Designer: Matie Anne Patterson
Illustrator: Tom Barrett
Typesetter: In House
Publication Printer: Brown
Paper Manufacturer: S. D. Warren Co.

Title: LI (Newsday)
Art Director: Clifford Gardiner
Illustrator: Gary Viskuipic
Printer: Providence Gravure

Title: Playboy Magazine
Art Director: Arthur Paul
Designer: Bob Post
Illustrator: Brad Holland
Publication Printer: W. F. Hall

Title: The N.Y. Times
Art Director: Steve Heller
Illustrator: Brad Holland
Typesetter: The N.Y. Times
Publication Printer: The N.Y. Times

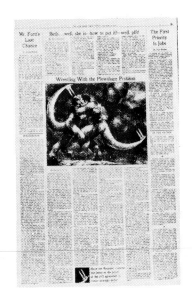

Title: Town & Country
Art Director: Ed Hamway
Designer: Ed Hamway
Illustrator: Robert Pryor
Publication Printer: Meredith

Title: National Lampoon
Designer: Peter Kleinman
Illustrator: Wayne McLoughlin
Typesetter: Haber Typographers, Inc.
Color Separator: Colorite
Publication Printer: Kansas Color Press

Title: Emergency Medicine
Art Directors: Ira Silberlicht, Tom Lennon
Designer: Tom Lennon
Ilustrator: Dickran Palulian
Typesetter: Allied Typographers, Inc.
Color Separator: Electronic Step and Repeat
Publication Printer: Perry Printing Corp.
Paper Manufacturer: Crown Zellerbach Corp.

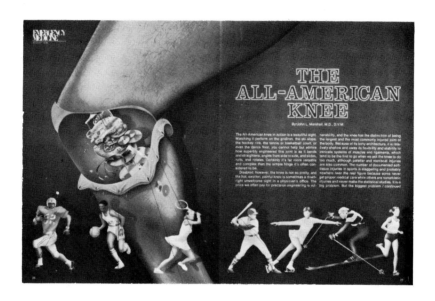

Title: Emergency Medicine
Art Directors: Ira Silberlicht, Tom Lennon
Designer: Tom Lennon
Illustrator: Geoffrey Moss
Typesetter: Allied Typographers, Inc.
Publication Printer: Perry Printing Corp.
Paper Manufacturer: Crown Zellerbach Corp.

Title: Medical Practice
Art Director: Burton P. Pollack
Designer: Elizabeth R. Cash
Illustrator: Jeff Cornell
Typesetter: Robert Guman/Photographic Productions
Separator: City Printing
Publication Printer: City Printing
Paper Manufacturer: Northwest

Title: Literary Cavalcade
Art Directors: Mary Zisk, Dale Moyer
Designer: Mary Zisk
Illustrator: David Palladini
Typesetter: Advanced Typographic Systems, Inc.
Color Separator: McCall's
Publication Printer: McCall's

Title: Companion
Art Director: Bernie Rotondo
Designer: Bernie Rotondo
Illustrator: Michael Steirnagle
Typesetter: RS Typographics
Color Separator: Lith-A-Tone
Publication Printer: Holiday Press
Paper Manufacturer: Crown Zellerbach

ARE YOU A WORKAHOLIC?

You may need to give yourself a break

Did you have a vacation this past summer? If you did, and enjoyed it without worrying about how the office was doing without you, that's a good indication that you have a normal (and healthy) attitude toward your job. Even if you did worry about the office, at least you did take a vacation. However, many sociologists, job counselors and management consultants point out that some executives are driving themselves too hard by insisting that they're too busy to take vacations. Many haven't taken a vacation in ten years. These are potential "workaholics," and these persons, according to the work experts interviewed for this article, are likely to take mental vacations on the job because of built-up stress and strain. To avoid creating workaholics, many companies are encouraging vacations for key personnel. For what makes the stress of tough, responsible work tolerable (even enjoyable) for the hard-driving executive or professional is the ability to control his time and take a vacation when he can.

Merry Christmas! Happy New Year! *Pssst!* And it's time, once a year, to step back from the brush strokes and look at the whole canvas. I often think of the lessons I have learned in aviation, they apply to much of life. An experienced pilot will never become fascinated with a single instrument, or allow his eyes to stay fixed on one other aircraft that may or may not be on a collision course, or permit his attention to remain concentrated for too long on a single aspect of his instrument clearance or some sudden problem in flight. Every minute or so, even when things are complicated, difficult, and getting raggedy, the pilot should relax his grip on the controls, sit back, take a deep breath, and go through the basic parameters of the flight, asking himself the basic questions: "Who am I? What is my aircraft number? Which direction should I be flying in? What is my assigned altitude? Which gas tank should I be on? What's my next radio fix, and my ETA for it? Has Center asked me to give them a report before then? How do I feel? Am I getting tired, or hypoxic?

Just so, in many situations in life you should step back for a moment, every so often, and ask if you've got the major structural elements put together right side up. Your investment program can

get out of whack, you know, and not always because you've made a mistake. The little trends can add up to anomalies after a while.

Suppose you made a speculation last year. It looked like a hot idea, but you were a prudent investor and you only put ten percent of your portfolio into it. Luck smiled upon you and that little speculation has quadrupled in price. If the rest of your portfolio stood still, you now have fully 30 percent of your market value in that little dog that you were scared to put more than 10 percent into last year. Take another look. Doctor. You may decide that you still don't want that much exposure. It may simply have been a lucky gambit. If so, take your profits, or a large portion of them, and run to the bank.

(I have done this once, and only once, for my own account. A friend, who was a partner in the investment house that was underwriting a new issue, told me they were going to give it a ride and offered me a charter membership. I put in some cash—ten percent of the total available at the time—and watched it quadruple in less than a year. I sold out completely and bought a new airplane with the proceeds. The stock sagged gradually, year after year, until the company went broke, and the stock went to exactly zero. But

the airplane flies like a dream.)

If you don't feel like bailing out completely, leave a little bit invested in the original position. But even this habit can lead to problems. After a few lucky turns you may have a portfolio bristling with minor positions in questionable ventures. The brica-brac may obscure the architecture. Clean house and start over.

Remind yourself of your basic objectives. Maybe you have some leftover positions that don't jibe with your current cash dividend. Maybe you have acquired some shares in a spin-off or picked up a few shares on the spur of a casual remark. Was your original intention to be 50-50 in stocks and bonds? Was your original objective an overall portfolio yield of six percent on market value—or six percent on cost or purchase price? Were you originally afraid to commit yourself to common stocks because you didn't like the idea of investing during an election year? Now that the elections are behind us, has the forward visibility improved enough for you to take a position in common stocks? If not, what's your fear now? Is the fear reasonable?

A review of your holdings may remind you that you sold your gold stocks for a tax-loss a year ago and haven't got around to moving back into golds. Is this

Continued on page 68 ▶

Every so often, you should step back and ask if you've got the major structural elements of your investment program put together right. Your portfolio can get out of whack, and not always because you've made a mistake. The little trends can add up to anomalies after a while.

BACK TO BASICS

Finance
by
William F. Rickenbacker

Title: Private Practice
Art Director: Michael Redwine
Illustrator: Lyle L. Miller
Typesetter: Ed-Be, Inc. OKL
Color Separator: Globe Color, OKL
Publication Printer: Mid-America Webpress
Paper Manufacturer: St. Regis

Title: Oui
Art Director: Don Menell
Designer: Jean-Pierre Holley
Illustrator: Emily Kaufman (sculptor)
Publication Printer: World Color Press

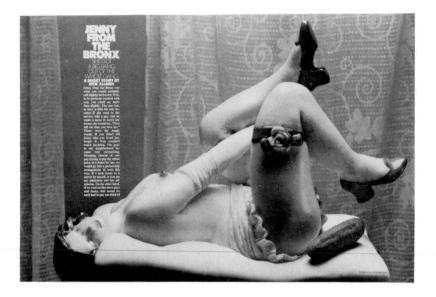

Title: Oui
Art Director: Don Menell
Designer: Jean-Pierre Holley

Illustrator: Tom Adams
Publication Printer: World Color Press

Title: Oui
Art Director: Don Menell
Designer: Michael Brock
Illustrator: Julian Allen
Publication Printer: World Color Press

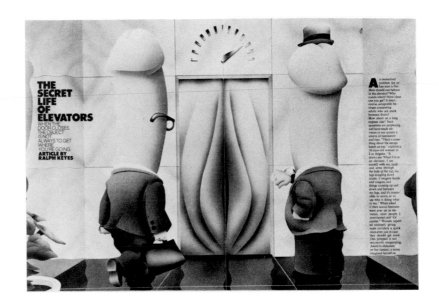

Title: Oui
Art Director: Don Menell
Designer: Don Menell

Illustrator: Robert Grossman
Printer: World Color Press

Title: Oui
Art Director: Don Menell
Designer: Jean-Pierre Holley
Illustrator: Guy Fery
Printer: World Color Press

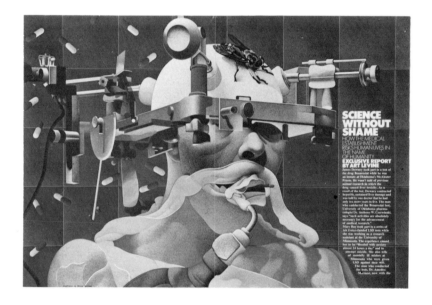

Title: Oui
Art Director: Don Menell
Designer: Don Menell

Illustrator: Wilson McLean
Publication Printer: World Color Press

Title: Rolling Stone
Art Director: Roger Black
Designer: Greg Scott
Ilustrator: Greg Scott
Typesetter: Mackenzie & Harris
Publication Printer: Mid-America Printing

Title: Sunday News Magazine
Art Director: Robert Clive
Designer: Thomas P. Ruis
Illustrator: Marcos Oksenhendler

Typesetter: NY News
Color Separator: N.Y. News
Publication Printer: N.Y. News

Title: The N.Y. Times Magazine
Art Director: Ruth Ansel
Designer: Anita Siegal
Photographer: N.Y. Times
Color Separator: N.Y. Times

Title: Nursing '76   **Typesetter:** In-House Merganthaler
Art Director: John Isely   **Publication Printer:** Brown
Designer: John Isely   **Paper Manufacturer:** S. D. Warren
Illustrator: Carl Nicholason

Title: Sunday News Magazine
Art Director: Robert Clive
Designer: Robert Clive
Illustrator: Michael Colton
Photographer: Edmund Peters
Typesetter: N.Y. News
Color Separator: N.Y. News
Publication Printer: N.Y. News

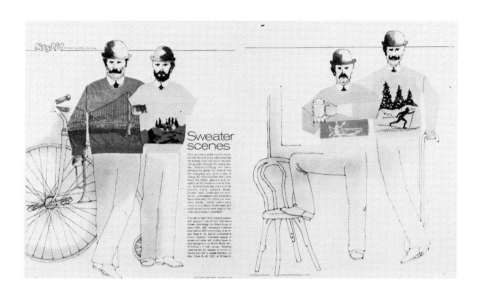

Title: Quest 77
Art Director: Noel Werrett
Designer: B. Martin Pedersen
Illustrator: Nicholas Gaetano
Typesetter: Cardinal Type Service
Color Separator: R. R. Donnelly
Publication Printer: R. R. Donnelly
Paper Manufacturer: Westvaco

Title: McCall's
Art Director: Modesto Torre
Designer: Bruno Blazina
Illustrator: Linda Gist

Title: New York
Art Directors: Walter Bernard, Milton Glaser
Designer: Walter Bernard
Illustrator: Paul Giovanopoulos

Title: Sky
Art Director: Ray Yee
Designer: Alan Cober
Typesetter: RS Typographics
Color Separator: Roberts Graphic Arts, Inc.
Publication Printer: Arcadia Graphics—Pacific Press
Paper Manufacturer: Crown Zellerbach

Title: New York
Art Directors: Walter Bernard, Milton Glaser
Designer: Walter Bernard
Illustrator: Julian Allen

Title: U & lc
Art Director: Herb Lubalin
Designer: Herb Lubalin
Illustrator: Jerome Snyder
Typesetter: M. J. Baumwell
Printer: Lincoln Graphic Arts, Inc.
Paper Manufacturer: Great Northern

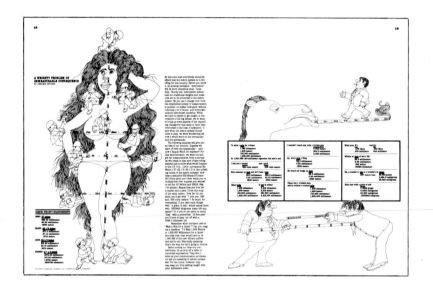

Title: Mainliner
Art Director: Chris Mossman
Designer: Chris Mossman
Illustrator: Jim Endicott
Typesetter: RS Typographics
Color Separator: Lithatone
Publication Printer: Deseret
Paper Manufacturer: Zellerbach

Title: New Times
Art Director: Steve Phillips
Designer: Steve Phillips
Illustrator: Vince Topazio
Typesetter: Typros & Unitron
Color Separator: Magnacolor
Publication Printer: R. R. Donnelley

Mainlining the Mexican revolution

By Lawrence Wright

handling the hand

By Ira M. Dusholt, M.D.

Title: Emergency Medicine
Art Directors: Ira Silberlicht, Tom Lennon
Designer: Tom Lennon
Illustrator: Nick Aristovolus
Photographer: Phil Gottheil
Typesetter: Allied Typographers, Inc.
Color Separator: Electronic Step and Repeat
Publication Printer: Perry Printing Corp.
Paper Manufacturer: Crown Zellerbach Corp.

Title: Emergency Medicine
Art Directors: Ira Silberlicht, Tom Lennon
Designer: Tom Lennon
Illustrator: Barbara Bascove
Typesetter: Allied Typographers, Inc.
Color Separator: Electronic Step and Repeat
Publication Printer: Perry Printing Corp.
Paper Manufacturer: Crown Zellerbach Corp.

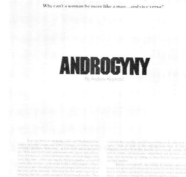

Title: New Times
Art Director: Steve Phillips
Designer: Steve Phillips
Illustrator: Carole Jean
Photographer: Steve Phillips
Typesetter: Typros & Unitron
Color Separator: Magnacolor
Publication Printer: R. R. Donnelley

Title: Emergency Medicine
Art Directors: Ira Silberlicht, Tom Lennon
Designer: Tom Lennon
Illustrator: Richard Krepel
Typesetter: Allied Typographers, Inc.
Color Separator: Electronic Step and Repeat
Publication Printer: Lincoln Graphic Arts, Inc.
Paper Manufacturer: Crown Zellerbach Corp.

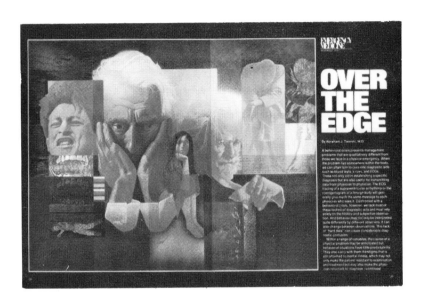

Title: Nursing '76
Art Director: John Isely
Designer: John Isely
Illustrator: John Dawson
Typesetter: In House VIP Mergenthaler
Color Separator: Litho Prep
Publication Printer: Brown
Paper Manufacturer: S. D. Warren

Title: Playboy
Art Director: Artuhr Paul
Designer: Bob Post
Illustrator: David Wilcox
Publication Printer: W. F. Hall

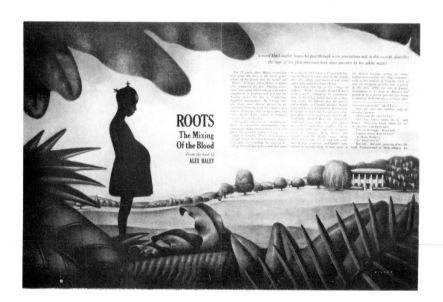

Title: Emergency Medicine
Art Directors: Ira Silberlicht, Tom Lennon
Designer: Tom Lennon
Illustrator: Randall Enos
Typesetter: Allied Typographers, Inc.
Publication Printer: Perry Printing Corp.
Paper Manufacturer: Crown Zellerbach Corp.

Title: Playboy
Art Director: Arthur Paul
Designer: Roy Moody
Illustrator: Chet Jezierski
Publication Printer: W. F. Hall

**HERBERT WARREN WIND'S
REFLECTIONS ON THE MASTERS**

Title: Golf Digest   **Typesetter:** J & J Typesetters
Art Director: John Newcomb   **Color Separator:** Toppan Printing
Designer: John Newcomb   **Publication Printer:** World Color Press
Illustrator: Bernie Fuchs

Title: Iron Age
Art Director: Jim Naughton
Designer: Trez Cattie
Illustrator: Ed Feldman
Typesetter: Chilton
Color Separator: Gilbert Color
Publication Printer: Chilton Printing
Paper Manufacturer: Champion

Title: Field & Stream   **Typesetter:** Boro Typographers/Printers Service Co., Inc.
Art Director: Victor J. Closi   **Color Separator:** Graphic Color Plate Inc.
Designer: Victor J. Closi   **Publication Printer:** Baird Ward Printing
Illustrator: Bob Kuhn   **Paper Manufacturer:** International & Consolidated

Title: The Arthur Young Journal
Art Director: David Starwood
Designer: David Starwood
Illustrator: John Hamberger
Typesetter: Johnson/Kenro, Boro
Publication Printer: S. D. Scott

Title: Playboy
Art Director: Arthur Paul
Designers: Arthur Paul, Kerig Pope
Illustrator: Dennis Michael Magdich
Publication Printer: W. F. Hall

Title: Teacher
Art Director: Vincent Ceci
Designer: Vincent Ceci
Illustrators: 4th Graders, Bedford Intermediate School, Pa.
Typesetter: Rumford Press
Color Separator: O'Brien Photo Engraving
Publication Printer: Rumford Press
Paper Manufacturer: Fraser

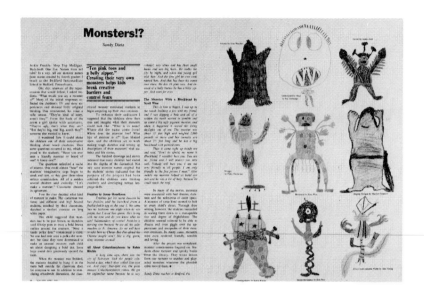

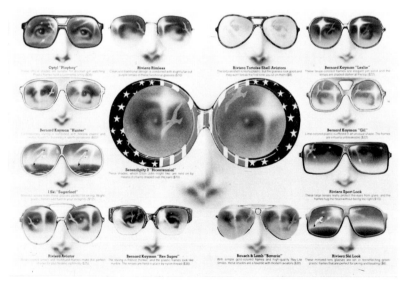

Title: Oui
Art Director: Don Menell
Designer: Michael Brock

Illustrator: Wayne McLoughlin
Publication Printer: World Color Press

Illustration — Story Presentation

Title: Playboy
Art Director: Arthur Paul
Designers: Arthur Paul, Kerig Pope
Illustrator: Dennis Michael Magdich
Publication Printer: W. F. Hall

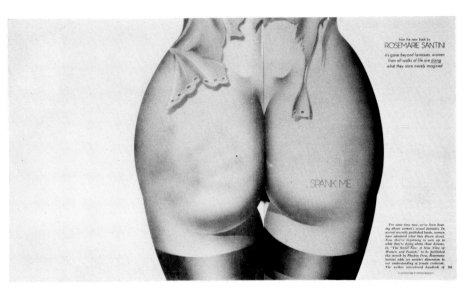

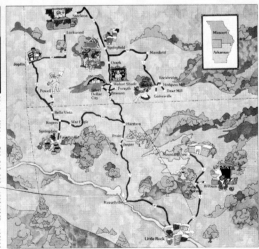

Title: Adventure Road
Art Director: Earl Glass
Designer: Dale DeBolt
Illustrator: James Conahan
Photographer: William Childress

Typesetter: R. R. Donnelley and Sons
Color Separator: R. R. Donnelley and Sons
Publication Printer: R. R. Donnelley and Sons
Paper Manufacturer: Nitec Corporation

Illustration — Story Presentation

Title: Psychology Today
Art Director: Neil Shakery
Designer: Noel Werrett
Illustrator: Robert Pryor
Publication Printer: Meredith

Title: Tempo
Art Director: Tom Burns Associates
Designer: John Urban
Illustrator: Eugene Mihaesco
Typesetter: VA Graphics
Publication Printer Davis-Delaney-Arrow
Paper Manufacturer: Mead Corp.

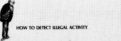

HOW TO DETECT ILLEGAL ACTIVITY

A Response to Corporate Fraud

HOW TO DEFINE THE LIMITS OF RESPONSIBILITY
by CARLETON H. GRIFFIN

Title: New York
Art Directors: Walter Bernard, Milton Glaser
Designer: Walter Bernard
Illustrator: James McMullan

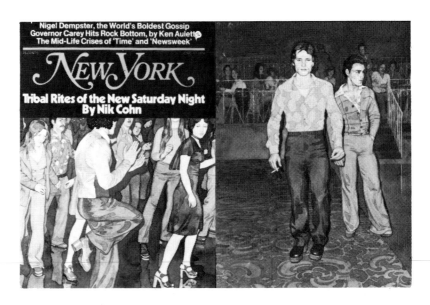

Title New York
Art Directors Walter Bernard; Milton Glaser
Designer: Walter Bernard
Illustrator: Harvey Dinnerstein

Illegal Immigrants in New York: The Invisible Subculture

By Orde Coombs

"...The illegal alien learns that to lie is to survive, that laws are made to be broken, that deviousness is the passport to success..."

"...Joyce is happy tonight because she thinks that with all the partying, Theo will get drunk and spend the weekend with her..."

Title: Potomac
Art Directors: Robert Barkin, David Moy
Designer: Robert Barkin
Illustrator: Geoffrey Moss
Typesetter: Wash. Post—Handwork: R. Barkin
Color Separator: Standard Gravure
Publication Printer: Standard Gravure

RAYS

Lurking in the Video, Rising from the Cathode Crypt . . .

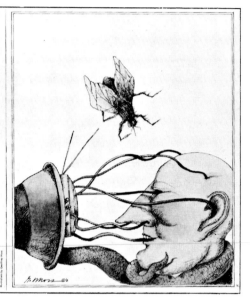

Fiction by Joel Swerdlow and Frank Mankiewicz

Alan Gutman woke up at 5:00 a.m. with a tight knot in his stomach. Not for far behind came waves of reassurance, reminders that this was the morning he had decided to share his convictions with a friend.

Title: Rolling Stone
Art Director: Roger Black
Designer: Roger Black
Illustrator: Ralph Steadman
Typesetter: Mackenzies & Harris
Publication Printing: Mid-America Printing

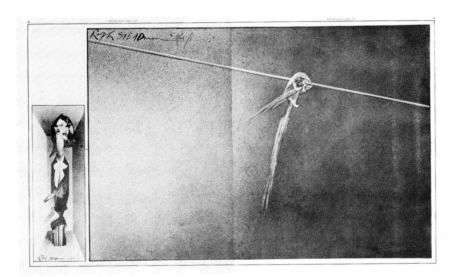

Title: Horizon
Art Director: Ken Munowitz
Designer: Ken Munowitz
Illustrator: Geoffrey Moss
Typesetter: The Composing Room of New England
Publication Printer: W. A. Krueger
Paper Manufacturer: Allied Paper Co.

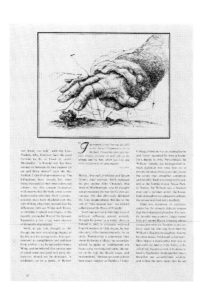

Title: Review
Art Director: Einar Vinje
Designer: Don Weller
Illustrator: Don Weller
Typesetter: RS Typographics/Headliners L.A.
Color Separator: Roberts Graphic Arts
Publication Printer: A. D. Weiss
Paper Manufacturer: Crown-Zellerback

Title: Mainliner
Art Director: Chris Mossman
Designer: Kathy Philpott
Illustrator: Jim Endicott
Typesetter: RS Typographics
Color Separator: Lithatone
Publication Printer: Deseret
Paper Manufacturer: Zellerbach

Title: The Lamp
Art Director: Harry O. Diamond
Designer: Harry O. Diamond
Illustrator: AB Nordbok-Goteborg, Sweden
Typesetter: Tri-Arts Press, Inc.
Color Separator: The Case-Hoyt Corporation
Publication Printer: The Case-Hoyt Corporation
Paper Manufacturer: Warren Paper Co.

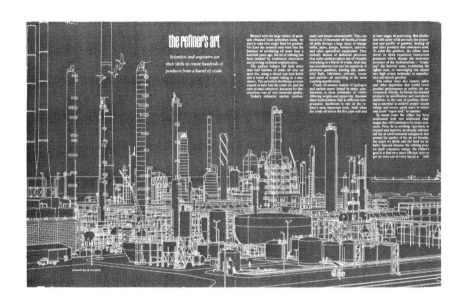

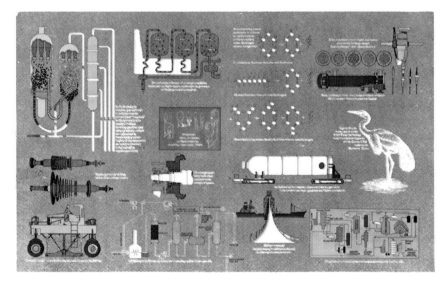

Title: U & lc
Art Director: Herb Lubalin
Designer: Herb Lubalin
Illustrator: Jerome Snyder
Typesetter: Photo Lettering Inc.
Publication Printer: Lincoln Graphic Arts, Inc.
Paper Manufacturer: Great Northern

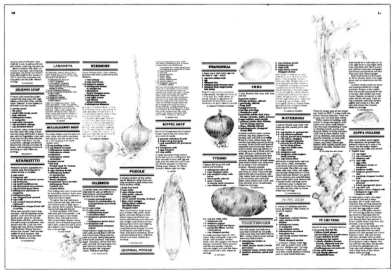

Title: U & lc
Art Director: Herb Lubalin
Designer: Herb Lubalin
Illustrator: Geoffrey Moss
Typesetter: M. J. Baumwell
Publication Printer: Lincoln Graphic Arts, Inc.
Paper Manufacturer: Great Northern

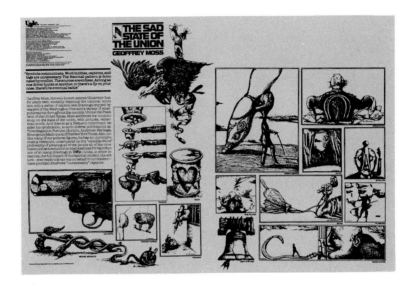

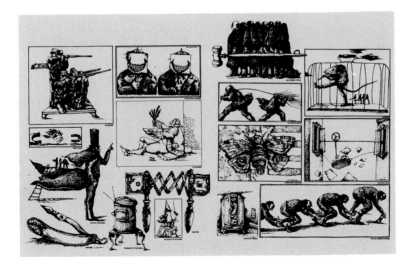

Title: Chicago
Art Director: Jack Lund
Designer: Bill Lowry
Illustrator: Arn Arnam
Typesetter: WFMT, Inc.Photofont
Color Separator: Viking
Publication Printer: Photopress

GANGLANDMARKS

by Connie Fletcher

Illustrations by Arn Arnam

Title: Horticulture
Art Director: Bruce McIntosh
Designer: Bruce McIntosh
Photographer: Marie Cosindas
Typesetter: Publishers' Design and Production Services
Color Separator: Andy Mowbray Inc.
Publication Printer: R. R. Donnelley
Paper Manufacturer: Blandin

Title: Horticulture
Art Director: Bruce McIntosh
Designer: Bruce McIntosh
Photographer: Alfred Eisenstaedt

Typesetter: Composing Room
Color Separator: Andy Mowbray Inc.
Publication Printer: R. R. Donnelley
Paper Manufacturer: Blandin

Title: Datamation
Art Director: Cleve Marie Boutell
Designer: Barbara Vada Benson
Photographer: Barbara Vada Benson
Typesetter: Continental Graphics
Color Separator: Color Service Corp.
Publication Printer: Beslow Assocs..

Title: Sunday News Magazine
Art Director: Robert Clive
Designer: Robert Clive
Photographer: Tom Arma

Title: The Lamp
Art Director: Harry O. Diamond
Designer: Harry O. Diamond
Photographer: David Moore
Typesetter: Tri-Arts Press, Inc.
Color Separator: The Case-Hoyt Corporation
Printer: The Case-Hoyt Corporation
Paper Manufacturer: Warren Paper Company

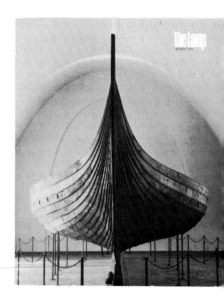

Title: RN Magazine
Art Directors: Albert M. Foti
Designer: JoAnne Cassella
Photographer: Jerry Sarapochiello
Typesetter: Arrow Typographers
Color Separator: G & S Litho
Publication Printer: Brown Printing
Paper Manufacturer: Mead

Title: RN Magazine
Art Directors: Albert M. Foti
Designer: JoAnne Cassella
Photographer: David Wagner
Typesetter: Arrow Typographers
Color Separator: G & S Litho
Publication Printer: Brown Printing
Paper Manufacturer: Mead

Title: RN Magazine
Art Directors: Albert M. Foti
Designer: JoAnne Cassella
Photographer: David Wagner
Typesetter: Arrow Typographers
Color Separator: G & S Litho
Publication Printer: Brown Printing
Paper Manufacturer: Mead

Title: Kiwanis
Art Director: Jane E. Bushwaller
Designer: Jane E. Bushwaller
Photographer: Frank Scholl
Color Separator: Progressive Graphics
Publication Printer: Mid America Webpress

Title: Modern Railroads
Art Director: John Wetzel
Photographer: John Wetzel
Color Separator: Direct Color
Publication Printer: Morton

Title: AIA Journal
Art Director: Suzy Thomas
Designer: Suzy Thomas
Photographer: Patricia Duncan
Typesetter: Hodges
Color Separator: Falcon
Printer: Judd & Detweiler
Paper Manufacturer: Westvaco

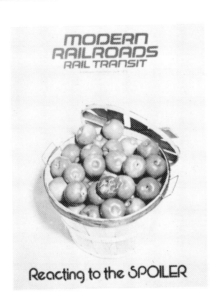

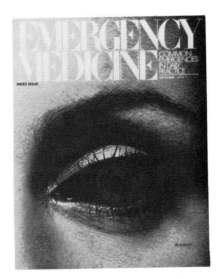

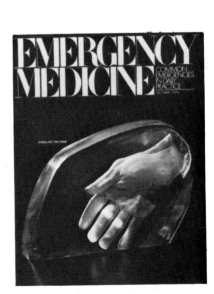

Title: Emergency Medicine
Art Directors: Ira Silberlicht, Tom Lennon
Designer: Tom Lennon
Illustrator: Judith Jampel
Photographer: Eugenia Louis
Typesetter: Allied Typographers, Inc.
Color Separator: Electronic Step and Repeat
Printer: Perry Printing Corp.
Paper Manufacturer: Crown Zellerbach

Title: Emergency Medicine
Art Directors: Ira Silberlicht, Tom Lennon
Designers: Tom Lennon, Irving J. Cohen
Photographer: Shig Ikeda
Typesetter: Allied Typographers, Inc.
Color Separator: Electronic Step Repeat
Publication Printer: Lincoln Graphic Arts
Paper Manufacturer: Crown Zellerbach

Title: Emergency Medicine
Art Directors: Ira Silberlicht, Tom Lennon
Designer: Tom Lennon
Illustrator: Nick Aristovulos
Photographer: Phil Gottheil
Typesetter: Allied Typographers Inc.
Color Separator: Electronic Step and Repeat
Publication Printer: Perry Printing Corp.
Paper Manufacturer: Crown Zellerbach

233

Title: New York
Art Directors: Walter Bernard, Milton Glaser
Designers: Walter Bernard, Tom Bentkowski
Photographer: Charles Wiesenhahn

Title: New York
Art Directors: Walter Bernard, Milton Glaser
Designer: Walter Bernard
Photographer: Dan Wynn

Title: New York
Art Directors: Walter Bernard, Milton Glaser
Designers: Walter Bernard, Tom Bentkowski
Photographer: Dan Wynn
Color Separator: Colliers

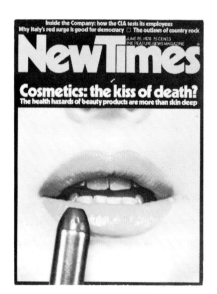

Title: New Times
Art Director: Steve Phillips
Designer: Steve Phillips
Photographer: Bill King
Typesetter: Typros
Color Separator: Magnacolor
Publication Printer: R. R. Donnelley

Title: These Times
Art Director: Gail R. Hunt
Designer: Gail R. Hunt
Photographer: David Damer
Typesetter: Southern Publishing Association
Color Separator: Southern Publishing Association
Publication Printer: Southern Publishing Association
Paper Manufacturer: Cordage of Nashville

Title: New Times
Art Director: Steve Phillips
Designer: Steve Phillips
Photographer: Carl Fischer
Typesetter: Typros
Color Separator: Magnacolor
Publication Printer: R. R. Donnelley

Title: Machine Design
Art Director: Ray Beckman
Designer: Ray Beckman
Photographer: Tim Ryan, Ryan Studios
Color Separator: Cleveland Engraving
Publication Printer: Pelton/IPC

Title: Psychology Today
Art Director: Neil Shakery
Designer: Neil Shakery
Photographer: Frank Maresca
Color Separator: Colins, Millet & Hutchings
Publication Printer: Meredith

Title: Progressive Architecture
Art Director: George W. Coderre
Photographer: David A. Morton
Publication Printer: W. A. Krueger

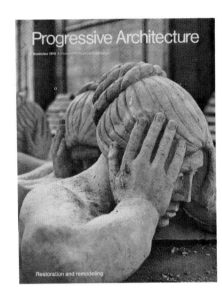

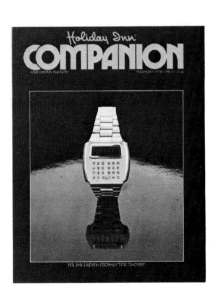

Title: Companion
Art Director: Chris Mossman
Photographer: Jim Cornfield
Typesetter: RS Typographics
Color Separator: Lith-A-Tone
Publication Printer: Holiday Press
Paper Manufacturer: Crown Zellerbach

Title: People
Art Director: Robert N. Essman
Designer: Robert N. Essman
Photographer: Douglas Kirkland
Typesetter: Gerard Associates
Color Separator: Graphic Color Plate
Publication Printer: Regensteiner

Title: Companion
Art Director: Sharon Sands-Fraser
Designer: Sharon Sands-Fraser
Photographer: Jim Cornfield
Typesetter: RS Typographics
Color Separator: Lithatone
Publication Printer: Holiday Press
Paper Manufacturer: Crown Zellerbach

Title: Clinical Laboratorian
Art Directors: Albert M. Foti, Thomas Phon
Designer: Thomas Phon
Photographer: Steve Eisenberg
Typesetter: Medical Economics Company
Color Separator: G & S Litho
Publication Printer: Mack Printing
Paper Manufacturer: Mead Paper Co.

Title: Medical Economics
Art Directors: Albert M. Foti, William J. Kuhn
Designer: Albert M. Foti
Photographer: Bob Weir
Typesetter: Arrow Typographers
Color Separator: Brown Printing
Publication Printer: Brown Printing
Paper Manufacture: Champion Paper Co.

Title: The Lamp
Art Director: Harry O. Diamond
Designer: Harry O. Diamond
Photographer: Co Rentmeester
Typesetter: Tri-Arts Press. Inc.
Color Separator: The Case-Hoyt Corporation
Printer: The Case-Hoyt Corporation
Paper Manufacturer: Warren Paper Co.

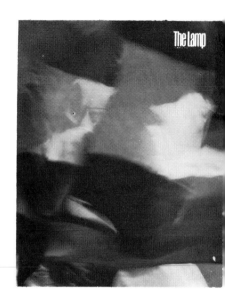

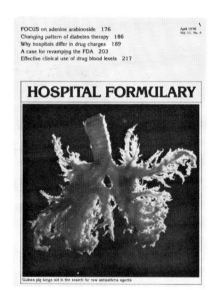

Title: Hospital Formulary
Art Directors: Phillip Dykstra, Peter Thiel
Photographer: Fritz Goro
Typesetter: Computer Graphics, Inc.
Color Separator: Colorhouse Inc.
Publication Printer: Hart Press
Paper Manufacturer: Westvaco

Title: Mainliner
Art Director: Bernie Retondo
Designer: Bernie Retondo
Photographer: Tommy Mitchell
Color Separator: Uthatone
Publication Printer: Deseret
Paper Manufacturer: Zellerbach

Title: Agri Marketing
Art Director: Phyllis Kaplan Barbieri
Designer: Phyllis Kaplan Barbieri
Photographer: Dick Kaplan
Typesetter: Phyllis Kaplan Barbieri
Color Separator: Quasar Graphics
Publication Printer: St. Croix Press Inc.
Paper Manufacturer: Warren

Title: Insight
Art Director: Byron Steele
Designer: Byron Steele
Illustrator: Salvador Bru
Color Separator: Review & Herald
Publication Printer: Review & Herald
Paper Manufacturer: Finch

Title: Clinical Bulletin
Art Director: Lynn McDowell
Designer: Lynn McDowell
Photographer: George Uibell, Ryon-Uibell
Publication Printer: Robert C. Gold Assoc
Paper Manufacturer: Northwest Paper

Title: Forbes
Art Director: Ed Wergeles
Designer: Ed Wergeles
Photographer: Francekevitch and Cobb
Typesetter: Franklin Typographers
Color Separator: Collier
Publication Printer: Dayton Press
Paper Manufacturer: Mead Paper

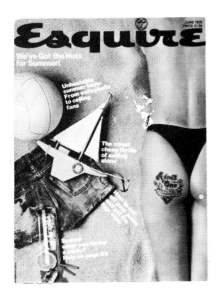

Title: Esquire
Art Director: Michael Gross
Designer: Michael Gross
Photographer: Arky & Barrett
Typesetter: Cardinal Typographers
Color Separator: R. R. Donnelley
Publication Printer: R. R. Donnelly

Title: Sail
Art Director: Robert Schroeder
Designer: Robert Schroeder
Photographer: Dan Nerney
Color Separator: Mowbray Co.
Publication Printer: R. R. Donnelley

Title: Sail
Art Director: Robert Schroeder
Designer: Robert Schroeder
Photographer: Steve Wilkings
Color Separator: Unigraphics
Publication Printer: R. R. Donnelley

Photography—Single Page

Title: New York News Magazine
Art Director: Robert Clive
Designer: Thomas P. Ruis
Photographer: Tom Arma
Typesetter: New York News
Color Separator: New York News
Printer: New York News

Title: Horticulture
Art Director: Bruce McIntosh
Designer: Bruce McIntosh

Title: New York
Art Directors: Walter Bernard, Milton Glaser
Designer: Walter Bernard
Photographer: Carl Fischer
Color Separator: Toppan

Title: Sunday News Magazine
Art Director: Robert Clive
Designer: Thomas P. Ruis
Photographer: Tom Arma

Title: Mainliner
Art Director: Chris Mossman
Designer: Kathy Philpott
Photographer: Jim Cornfield
Typesetter: RS Typographics & Computer Typesetting Ser-
Color Separator: Lithatone
Publication Printer: Deseret
Paper Manufacturer: Zellerbach

Title: Esquire
Art Director: Michael Gross
Designer: Jane Prettyman
Photographer: Ryszard Horowitz
Typesetter: Cardinal Typographers
Color Separator: R. R. Donnelley & Sons
Publication Printer: R. R. Donnelley & Sons

Title: People
Art Director: Robert N. Essman
Designer: Sanae Yamazaki
Typesetter: Time Inc. Videocomp
Publication Printer: R. R. Donnelley
    - Pacifica Press

Title: Quest/77
Art Director: Noel Werrett
Designer: Noel Werrett
Photographer: Peter Angelo Simon

Typesetter: Cardinal
Color Separator: R. R. Donnelley
Publication Printer: R. R. Donnelley
Paper Manufacturer: Westvaco

Title: These Times
Art Director: Gail R. Hunt
Designer: Gail R. Hunt
Photographer: David Damer
Typesetter: Southern Publishing
Color Separator: Southern Publishing
Publication Printer: Southern Publishing
Paper Manufacturer: Cordage of Nashville

Title: Family Circle
Art Director: John Bradford
Designer: Teresa Montalvo
Photographer: Gordon E. Smith
Typesetter: Haber
Color Separator: R. R. Donnelley
Publication Printer: R. R. Donnelley

transcendental meditation

by Ken McFarland

Is transcendental meditation the universally sought elixir for all life's problems, from simple nervous tension to psychosomatic illness? Or is it a Hindu wolf in an American sheepskin?

Title: New York
Art Directors: Walter Bernard, Milton Glaser
Designer: Walter Bernard
Photographer: Carl Fischer
Color Separator: Colliers

Title: Sundancer
Art Director: Cliff Wynne
Designer: Cliff Wynne
Photographer: Jim Cornfield

Typesetter: Computer Typesetting
Color Separator: Angel Color
Publication Printer: Pacific Press
Paper Manufacturer: Crown Zellerbach

240

Title: New Times
Art Director: Steve Phillips
Photographer: Carl Fischer
Typesetter: Typros & Unitron
Color Separator: Magnacolor
Publication Printer: R. R. Donnelley

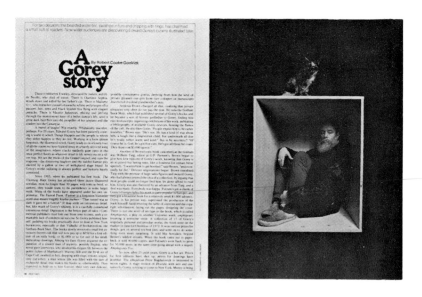

Title: People
Art Director: Robert N. Essman
Designer: Sanae Yamazaki
Photographer: Curt Gunther, Camera 5
Typesetter: Time Inc. - Videocomp
Publication Printer: R. R. Donnelley - Pacifica Press

Title: Industry Week
Art Director: Chris J. Nehlen
Designers: Chris Nehlen, Jacqueline Kohn
Photographer: J. David Wilder
Typesetting: Penton Press
Color Separator: Staufer Litho
Publication Printer: Penton Press

Most couples find ways to adjust to the pressures two careers can put on a marriage. But transfers, travel, and long hours on the job present difficulties in even the most successful relationships.

Problems of dual-career marriages

By Vivian C. Pospisil

The ghost of campaigns past continues to haunt the Democratic race. The question is, has the junior senator from Minnesota blown his timing once again?

THE VERY LAST HURRAH OF HUBERT HORATIO HUMPHREY

By Robert Sam Anson

Title: New Times
Art Director: Steve Phillips
Designer: Steve Phillips
Photographer: David Burnett
Typesetter: Typros & Unitron
Color Separator: Magnacolor
Publication Printer: R. R. Donnelley

Photography—Single Spread

Title: Emergency Magazine
Art Directors: Ira Silberlicht, Tom Lennon
Designer: Tom Lennon
Photographer: Shig Ikeda
Typesetter: Allied Typographers, Inc
Color Separator: Electronic Step and Repeat
Publication Printer: Perry Printing Corp
Paper Manufacturer: Crown Zellerbach Corp

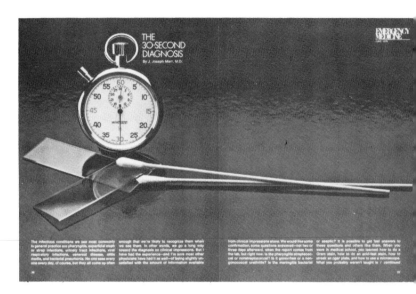

Title: Town & Country
Art Director: Ed Hamway
Designer: Brad Pallas
Photographer: Michel Tcherevkoff

Color Separator: National Bickford Graphics, Inc.
Publication Printer: Meredith Printing Corp.

Title: PSA California
Art Director: Cliff Wynne
Designer: Cliff Wynne
Photographer: Jim Cornfield
Typesetter: Computer Typesetting
Publication Printer: Pacific Press
Paper Manufacturer: Crown Zellerbach

A high-energy visit with a man who makes music

Taj

by Jessica Maxwell

time out

Windsurfing: 'A Physical Sport With a Lot of Mystique'

Title: Sports Medicine
Art Director: Tina Adamek
Designers: Steve Bloom, Greg Schultz
Photographer: Steve Wilkings

Title: New Times
Art Director: Steve Phillips
Designer: Steve Phillips
Photographer: Sandy Solmon
Typesetter: Typros & Unitron
Color Separator: Magnacolor
Publication Printer: R. R. Donnelley

MOSE ALLISON

By Robert Ward

HE DON'T WORRY 'BOUT A THING ('CAUSE EVERYTHING IS GOING TO BE ALRIGHT)

RUSSIAN EXTRAVAGANZA

Title: New York
Art Directors: Walter Bernard, Milton Glaser
Designer: Walter Bernard
Photographer: Bradley Olman

Title: New Times
Art Director: Steve Phillips
Designer: Steve Phillips
Photographer: Steve Phillips
Typesetter: Typros & Unitron
Color Separator: Magnacolor
Publication Printer: R. R. Donnelley

Title: Pepsi-Cola World
Art Director: Nancy C. Krieger
Designer: Nancy C. Krieger
Photographer: Dave G. Houser

Typesetter: Advertising Agencies Headliners
Publication Printer: DePerri Printing

Title: Emergency Magazine
Art Directors: Ira Silberlicht, Tom Lennon
Designer: Tom Lennon
Photographer: Shig Ikeda
Typesetter: Allied Typographers, Inc.
Color Separator: Electronic Step and Repeat
Publication Printer: Perry Printing Corp
Paper Manufacturer: Crown Zellerbach

Title: People
Art Director: Robert N. Essman
Designer: Robert N. Essman
Photographer: Declan Haun
Typesetter: Time Inc. Videocomp
Publication Printer: R. R. Donnelley - Pacifica Press

Title: Sundancer
Art Director: Cliff Wynne
Designer: Cliff Wynne
Photographer: Ron Shuman
Typesetter: Computer Typesetting Services
Color Separator: Angel Color
Publication Printer: Pacific Press
Paper Manufacturer: Crown Zellerbach

Title: New Times
Art Director: Steve Phillips
Designer: Steve Phillips
Photographer: Steve Phillips

Typesetter: Typros & Unitron
Color Separator: Magnacolor
Publication Printer: R. R. Donnelley

Title: New Times
Art Director: Steve Phillips
Designer: Steve Phillips
Photographer: Edie Baskin
Typesetter: Typros & Unitron
Color Separator: Magnacolor
Publication Printer: R. R. Donnelley

Title: Esquire
Art Director: Bob Ciano
Designer: Carla Barr
Illustrator: John O'Leary

Typesetter: Cardinal Typographers
Color Separator: R. R. Donnelley & Sons
Publication Printer: R. R. Donnelley & Sons

Title: Clipper
Art Director: Sharon Sands-Fraser
Designer: Sharon Sands-Fraser
Photographer: Michael Kuh
Typesetter: Garon Graphics
Color Separator: Roberts Graphic Arts
Publication Printer: Peninsula Lithograph Co.
Paper Manufacturer: Crown Zellerbach

by Peter Buckley

LA FAMILIA DOMECQ

Spain's greatest
producer of
the nation's
best wine

SURLYN VS. BALATA: WHICH SHOULD YOU PLAY? By LARRY DENNIS Associate Editor

Title: Gold Digest
Art Director: John Newcomb
Designer: Jerry Cosgrove
Photographer: Jerry Cosgrove
Typesetter: J & J Typesetters
Color Separator: Toppan Printing
Publication Printer: World Color Press

Title: Boston
Art Director: Ronn Campisi
Designer: Ronn Campisi
Photographer: John Crall
Typesetter: Publishers Design & Production Service
Publication Printer: Chilton

Title: Family Circle
Art Director: John Bradford
Designer: John Bradford
Photographer: Lynn St. John
Typesetter: Haber
Color Separator: R. R. Donnelley
Publication Printer: R. R. Donnelley

Title: New Times
Art Director: Steve Phillips
Designer: Steve Phillips
Photographer: Michel Tcherevkoff
Typesetter: Typros & Unitron
Color Separator: Magnacolor
Publication Printer: R. R. Donnelley

Today the strawberry, tomorrow...

By Ruth Rosenbaum

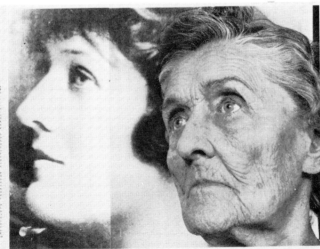

After the Ball

Fifty-seven years ago, at the Cho-Cho Ball, Edith Hyde Robbins became the first Miss America. Now she sits in her nursing home —and remembers.

BY WENDY THOMAS

Title: Sunday News Magazine
Art Director: Robert Clive
Designer: Robert Clive
Designer: Robert Clive
Photographer: Mel Finkelstein

Title: Clipper
Art Director: Sharon Sands-Fraser
Designer: Sharon Sands-Fraser
Photographer: Carla de Benedetti, Milan

Title: People
Art Director: Robert N. Essman
Designer: Robert N. Essman
Photographer: Harry Benson
Typesetter: Time Inc. Videocomp
Publication Printer: R. R. Donnelley - Pacifica Press

Title: New Times
Art Director: Steve Phillips
Designer: Steve Phillips
Photographer: Steve Phillips
Typesetter: Typros & Unitron
Color Separator: Magnacolor
Publication Printer: R. R. Donnelley

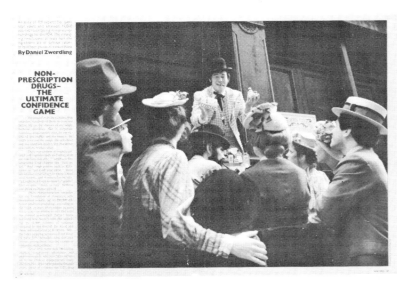

Title: Emergency Magazine
Art Directors: Ira Silberlicht, Tom Lennon
Designers: Tom Lennon, Irving J. Cohen
Photographer: Shig Ikeda
Typesetter: Allied Typographers, Inc.
Color Separator: Electronic Step and Repeat
Publication Printer: Lincoln Graphic Arts, Inc.
Paper Manufacturer: Crown Zellerbach Corp.

Photography — Story Presentation

Title: Sundancer
Art Director: Cliff Wynne
Designer: Cliff Wynne
Photographer: Jim Cornfield
Typesetter: Computer Typesetting Services
Color Separator: Angel Color
Publication Printer: Pacific Press
Paper Manufacturer: Crown Zellerbach

MADE IN AMERIKA

PLAY IT AGAIN, UNCLE SAM

by Leonard Feather

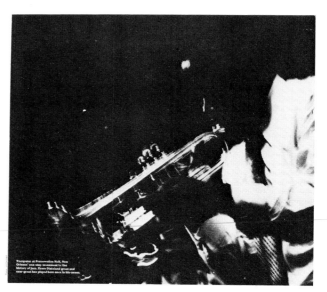

Trumpeter at Preservation Hall, New Orleans' one-stop monument to the history of jazz. Every Dixieland great and near great has played here since to his career.

The Olympia Brass Band plays for a traditional jazz funeral parade at St. Louis II cemetery.

Gospel sounds from the Zion Harmonizers.

Father Al, a New Orleans legend, still plucking his custom banjo after more than 50 years of playing with jazz's biggest names.

Title: Quest/77
Art Director: Noel Werrett
Designer: Noel Werrett
Photographer: Eva Rubinstein
Typesetter: Cardinal
Color Separator: R. R. Donnelley
Publication Printer: R. R. Donnelley
Paper Manufacturer: Westvaco

Title: Country Journal
Art Director: Thomas Morley
Designer: Thomas Morley
Photographer: Gregory Thorp
Typesetter: Atlantic Typographers
Color Separator: Chanticleer Co.
Publication Printer: Judd & Detweiler
Paper Manufacturer: St. Regis

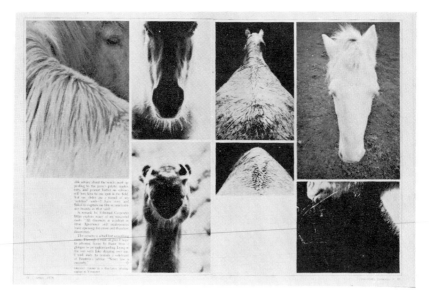

Title: New York
Art Directors: Walter Bernard, Milton Glaser
Designer: Joan Dworkin
Typesetter: Sterling

Color Separator: Toppan
Publication Printer: Arcata
Paper Manufacturer: Crown Zellerbach

Title: Home
Art Director: Hans Albers
Designer: Hans Albers
Photographer: Hans Albers
Color Separator: Alco-Gravure California Roto Gravure
   Division
Publication Printer: Alco-Gravure California Roto Gravure
   Division

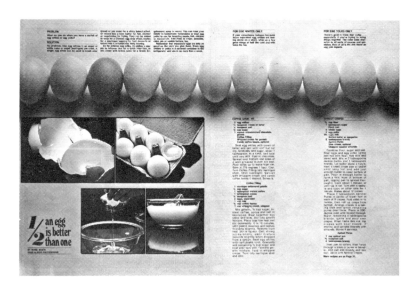

Title: Horizon
Art Director: Ken Munowitz
Designer: Ken Munowitz
Illustrator: Douglas Tyler
Photographer: Balthazar Korab

Typesetter: The Composing Room of New England
Color Separator: Chanticleer Press
Publication Printer: W. A. Krueger
Paper Manufacturer: Mead Paper Co.

Title: Chicago
Art Director: Jack Lund
Designer: Jack Lund
Photographer: Lucky Curtis
Typesetter: WFMT, inc
Color Separator: Viking Graphics
Publication Printer: Photopress

Title: Emergency Medicine
Art Directors: Ira Silberlicht, Tom Lennon
Designer: Tom Lennon
Illustrator: Judith Jampel
Photographer: Eugenia Louis
Typesetter: Allied Typographers, Inc.
Color Separator: Electronic Step and Repeat
Printer: Perry Printing Corp.
Paper Manufacturer: Crown Zellerbach Corp.

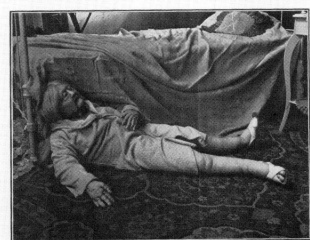

As strangers in the land

Old bones: action, not traction

Title: Horticulture
Art Director: Bruce McIntosh
Designer: Bruce McIntosh
Photographer: Carola Gregor
Typesetter: Composing Room
Color Separator: Andy Mowbray
Publication Printer: R. R. Donnelley
Paper Manufacturer: Blandin

Title: Town & Country
Art Director: Linda Stillman   **Photographer:** Silano
Designer: Brad Pallas   **Printer:** Meredith Printing Corp.

Title: Esquire
Art Director: Michael Gross
Designer: Jane Prettyman
Photographer: Maureen Lambray
Typesetter: Cardinal Typographers
Color Separator: R. F. Donnelley & Sons
Publication Printer: R. F. Donnelley & Sons

Title: Texas Monthly
Art Director: Jim Darilek
Designer: Jim Darilek
Photographer: Michael Patrick
Typesetter: G & S Typesetters
Color Separator: Wallace Engraving
Publication Printer: Texas Color Printer

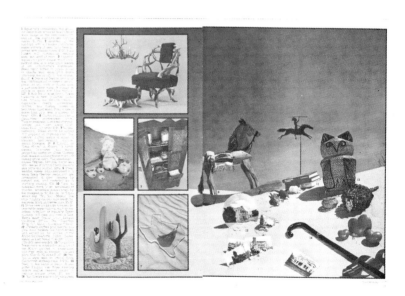

Title: The Lamp
Art Director: Harry O. Diamond
Designer: Harry O. Diamond
Photographers: David Moore, Harry O. Diamond, Fran
    Diamond, Ernest Dunbar

Typesetter: Tri-Arts Press, Inc.
Color Separator: The Case-Hoyt Corporation
Publication Printer: The Case-Hoyt Corporation
Paper Manufacturer: Warren Paper Co.

Title: New York
Art Directors: Walter Bernard, Milton Glaser
Designers: Walter Bernard, Tom Bentkowski
Photographer: Gianfranco Gorgoni, Contact
Color Separator: Colliers

Title: Oui
Art Director: Don Menell
Designer: Don Menell
Publication Printer: World Color Press

Title: Progressive Architecture
Art Director: George W. Coderre
Publication Printer: W. A. Krueger

Title: Horizon
Art Director: Ken Munowitz
Designer: Ken Munowitz
Photographer: Joseph Koudelka—Magnum
Typesetter: The Composing Room of New England
Publication Printer: W. A. Krueger
Paper Manufacturer: Mead Paper Co.

Title: Texas Monthly
Art Director: Sybil Broyles
Designer: Sybil Broyles
Photographers: Michael Patrick, Gary Bishop, Walter Nelson
Typesetter: G & S Typesetters
Color Separator: Wallace Engraving
Publication Printer: Texas Color Printer

Title: LI Magazine
Art Director: Clifford Gardiner
Photographers: Ken Spencer, Harvey Weber
Publication Printer: Providence Gravure

Title: Popular Photography
Art Director: Shinichiro Tora
Designer: Shinichiro Tora
Photographer: Grant Mudford

Title: Popular Photography
Art Director: Shinichiro Tora
Designer: Shinichiro Tora
Photographer: Ralph Gibson

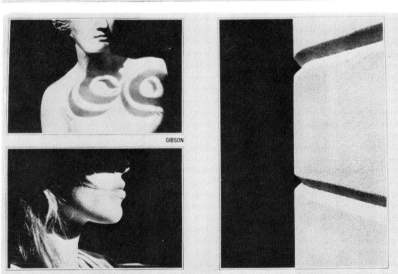

Title: Horticulture
Art Director: Bruce McIntosh
Designer: Bruce McIntosh
Photographer: Alfred Eisenstaedt

Eisenstaedt's Orchids

An intimate portrait of an exotic flower
Photographed by Alfred Eisenstaedt
Text by Gordon Dillon

YALE WORKERS

Title: Yale Alumni Magazine
Art Director: Nathan Garland
Designer: Nathan Garland
Photographer: Rodney Smith
Typesetter: Connecticut Printers, Inc.
Publication Printer: Connecticut Printers, Inc
Paper Manufacturer: St. Regis

Title: Sundancer
Art Director: Cliff Wynne
Designer: Cliff Wynne
Photographer: Gary Krueger
Typesetter: Computer Typesetting
Publication Printer: Pacific Press
Paper Manufacturer: Crown Zellerbach

ART DIRECTORS/DESIGNERS

ARTISTS & PHOTOGRAPHERS

TYPESETTERS

COLOR SEPARATORS

PRINTERS

PAPER MANUFACTURERS

PUBLICATIONS